Space Planning

Space Planning

Comprehensive Guide for
Residential Interior Space Planning

Lamie E.

Copyright © 2011 by Lamie E.

Library of Congress Control Number: 2011910873
ISBN: Hardcover 978-1-4628-9611-0
Softcover 978-1-4628-9610-3
Ebook 978-1-4628-9612-7

All rights reserved. No part of this book may be reproduced or transmitted in any form or by any means, electronic or mechanical, including photocopying, recording, or by any information storage and retrieval system, without permission in writing from the copyright owner.

This book was printed in the United States of America.

To order additional copies of this book, contact:
Xlibris Corporation
1-888-795-4274
www.Xlibris.com
Orders@Xlibris.com
85871

Contents

Foreword 7
Introduction 9

Chapter 1-Space Planning 13

Why Space Planning? 13
Residential Interior Space Planning 15
Elements and Principle of Design 16
Residential Interior Space Planning Process 20
Predesign 23
Design 30
Presentation 35

Chapter 2-Drafting 38

Basics of Drafting 38
Drawing Tools 46
Start to draw 55
Assignment no. 1: Line weight 57
Assignment no. 2: Use of scale 59
Start to Draw a Furniture Plan 59

Chapter 3-Accessible and Green Design 62

Accessible and Green 62
Green Design 63

Barrier-Free Design 68
Residential Requirements 72
Living room, family room, and dining room.............. 81

Chapter 4-Room by Room 82

Room by Room.. 82
Foyer 85
Powder Room 86
Home Office.. 88
Kitchen.. 90
Great Room/Family Room... 93
Formal Living Room 95
Dining Room 96
Bathroom 99
Laundry Room... 105
Children's Room 107
Master Bedroom... 110
Master Bedroom Suite 112
Put Everything Together... 115
Assignment Plans 115
The client: 116

Chapter 5-Final Project... 136

The Project... 136
The Challenges and the Solutions............................. 137

Solutions:.. 139
Refrences:... 144

Foreword

Having moved to Canada in 1999 with seventeen years of experience in architectural design, I started to study Interior Design which was one of the closest subjects to my background and a favorite field of mine. Taking many courses in BCIT (British Colombia Institute of Technology) gave me the confidence to start my own small business (St. Georges Interior) in Vancouver. Later I had the opportunity to start working as an instructor with "Choices Décor group," teaching two different courses. Space planning was one of them. I started to search for more resources, to study, to take notes, and to have my own manuscript for my teaching career. The idea of arranging this book started back then.

Couple of years later I realized no matter how experienced you are, it is necessary to have a diploma from one of the accredited schools in Canada. That is how I obtained my IDDP (International Design and Decorating professional) Diploma from QC school of design.

In early 2010, my husband and I moved to Calgary, and that is when I started to work on this book based on all the experiences gained from teachers and students, study, and practicing.

Introduction

Although this book is not for dummies, it can be an "easy to read and practice" guide for residential interior space planning which can be used by a variety of people who desire to learn about the subject.

If you are **a student in architectural or interior design and decorating school,** you will find this book attractive and useful as you will be able to obtain a systematic information process toward a successful space planning while you will have the chance to practice on a few different projects.

If you are a **non-English speaking professional** in design field who wants to refresh his/her knowledge about "space planning" in English, you will have an easy-to-follow source which will walk you through the subject.

If you want **to touch the basics of interior design and decorating** to see if you are interested in studying this field, you will finish this book with some basic drawing skills, a methodology for a successful "space planning," and a quick review of elements and principles of design which will give you the basic definition of design tools and the chance to review and work on a few projects.

If you are a **homeowner who needs some minor renovation or changes in interiors,** you can still use this book as a "do-by-yourself" guide.

If you are a **sales representative** in a furniture shop, you will get the knowledge you need to help your client and the chance to practice to be ready for different cases.

If you are a **realtor** who wants to appear more professional in front of clients by helping them improve their interior arrangement to sell the property faster, you will find it like a handbook with tangible samples to carry with you. Design wise, the vocabulary will make you confident to communicate efficiently.

And finally, if you are just **curious to know** what space planning is all about, you will have a source of basic definitions and rules to feed your curiosity.

No matter which group you belong to, you are supposed to leave this book with a better understanding and a basic knowledge of subjects listed below:

- The term "space planning" and the method for a successful one
- Elements and principles of design
- Basic drafting and drawing skill
- Ability to create an efficient space plan

- Preliminary knowledge of related subjects like barrier-free and green design which have a strong impact on today's design target.

Hope you will find it comprehensive and useful.

Good Luck!

Lamie

Chapter 1

Space Planning

Why Space Planning?

The word "efficient" means to work or operate quickly and effectively in an organized way.

Efficiency means that both time and energy are used well, without wasting any.

Efficiency is a word applied to just about everything designed to use whether a car a dishwasher or a space.

Lack of an efficient organization for home interiors will create a haphazard, nonfunctional space. As a result, the defined function of the space is not achievable through the existing organization or design.

That is why interior designers are increasingly using the popular word "efficient" to describe proper furniture arrangement. I believe space planning, as some people think, is not just furniture arrangement. The way we organize things in any space is called space planning, and even when you organize items in a single drawer, in fact you are entering the act of space planning for that particular space which in this example is the small inside space of a drawer.

The most efficient and functional home interior is achievable when all spaces from a single kitchen drawer to the biggest room are organized by using the principle of space planning.

It is understandable why without spatial consideration and keeping all the rules in mind, a few beautiful pieces of furniture can't create a wonderful interior even if they are located in the proper place and why space planning is not just furniture arrangement.

Space planning is an essential part of interior design and decorating, a series of actions, and definitely is a solid foundation for all actions which come later.

Residential interior space planning is an artistic professional skill which is involved with culture, lifestyle, and needs and wants of a person or a family who lives in that particular place.

There are even more details involved with space planning for people with any kind of disability or the fast-growing trend of green design. We will stay focused on residential space planning essentials, but we will have a quick review of these subjects to intrigue your desire to obtain more knowledge about each of them.

If you ask me whether we need space planning in a tent when out for camping, I would say, yes, if you want to use the space efficiently and to provide the highest level of comfort you need to think about it like a small space planning project.

The smart people who perceived the importance of space planning, established companies to organize one's home's garage or walking closet with some principle like functionality and balance in mind.

Talking about functionality and balance is a reminder that lack of requisite knowledge of elements and principles of design means having no tool for a disciplined design.

We will review these subjects as we are moving forward in our journey to be a successful space planner.

Residential Interior Space Planning

A strong foundation of knowledge about elements and principle of design is necessary to create a successful design.

These basic units of design and the relationship between them will act as your tools to work through space planning process to create the final product which is a successful design functionally and aesthetically.

Elements and Principle of Design

Design elements and principles describe fundamental ideas about the practice of a good, successful design. The elements shape the "vocabulary" of design and are basic set of tools to work with, while the principles are the structural aspects of its composition. These principles are used in all kind of designs, including interior design, graphic design, industrial design, web design, architecture, and fine art.

1-Elements of Design

Elements of design are line, form, texture, color, and space and are the basic units of a design.

Line

Line is the basic element that refers to the continuous movement of a drawing tool such as a pen, pencil, marker, or a brush.

Line can be horizontal, vertical, curved, diagonal, zigzag, or wavy. Although dashed and dotted lines are not the result of continuous movement of drawing tools, we still call them line.

Straight and curved lines are the basics of two-dimensional shapes like a house plan; lines have length, thickness, and direction.

Form (shape)

Form is the shape and structure of a dimensional element. Form can be both two-dimensional and three-dimensional. The terms "form" and "shape" are often used synonymously.

Texture

Texture is used to create surface appearance and often refers to the material that something is made of; texture is both a visual and a tactile phenomenon. Tactile means pleasant or attractive to touch.

Color

Color is the response of the eye to different wavelengths of radiation within the visible spectrum, thus there is no color without the light. It is told that color memory doesn't exist as the perceived color may be different by changing the amount and direction of the light on that particular surface.

What we can see as a color depends on hue, value, and saturation of the color.

Hue: Terms such as red, green, blue define the hue of a color.

Value: The general lightness or darkness of a color is the value of that particular color.

Saturation: It is the intensity of a color.

Space

Space is the area provided for a particular purpose. It may have two dimensions (length and width), such as a floor, or it may have three dimensions (length, width, and height) like a room.

2-Principle of Design

The principle of design talks about relationships of the elements used in design. Functionality, proportion, harmony, contrast, focal point, balance, and unity are mentioned here as principles of design while we are focused on interior design.

Functionality

The most important aspect of a good design is functionality which is the best possible design to support the lifestyle, needs, and wants of the occupants.

Creating the most beautiful space which does not serve the function is not acceptable as a good design.

Proportion

Proportion is the relationship of size between objects.

Harmony

Harmony in design is similarity of objects. When some of the objects like sofas and soft window treatments (drapes) share a common trait, we can describe them as harmonized objects.

Common trait between different things in a room can be: color, shape, texture, pattern, style, or size.

Contrast

It is the difference between size, color, texture of the objects and can create visual interest.

Very sharp contrast is able to attract lots of attention if there is any need for that.

Emphasis or focal point

Focal point refers to the areas of interest that guide the eyes into and make the space more attractive. Creating a focal point is a task to be done when space planning is needed.

Balance

Balance is a state where things are of equal weight or force or importance. Balance can be symmetrical or asymmetrical.

In a well-designed location, volume, or size, and the color of the objects create a sense of visual balance; a well-balanced interior usually is more comfortable.

Unity

In many texts written about design and also in my opinion, unity is the ultimate target for the design which refers to a sense that everything in a design belongs there to make the whole and is achievable by the use of design principles.

In another words, everything is working together to create the whole.

Residential Interior Space Planning Process

Babies grow up to become toddlers, toddlers will be teenagers, kids will move out, new home styles and trends are introduced, home office is needed, aging process calls for some adjustment . . . and there are hundred more reasons for a change in where we live.

A space planning process starts when a person, a family, or a group of people living in one building want or need to put the building or part of that to a new function or a new style.

To create a new building or to turn down an existing building to create a new one, a team of professionals, starting with an architect, is needed to work together, and it is different from what this book is trying to explain about residential interior space planning.

The intention to change, in spite of the reason to initiate the intention, will lead people to study about space planning to see what they can do by themselves or will bring up the idea of consulting with a professional in the field of design and décor.

If you are among the first group who wants to know about space planning to be able to change the furniture arrangement or to add or remove a few pieces in your place, I recommend you to study the elements and principle of design in order to have a better understanding about your path and your target to create a desirable ambience. Later, you can practice the bubble diagram and traffic pattern techniques; you may want to try the cutouts furniture to work on your plan to move the pieces a few times, then when you are satisfied, you can move, remove, or add the same items in your actual room which will save you time and the hassle of moving heavy pieces around. Even if you designed to move almost everything, at least you are prepared to ask for help, to schedule your time, and finally to do it in a one single attempt instead of having an untidy room for days and getting tired of these changes which will make you care less about some details and those little final touches.

On the other hand, to have a professional consultant is what some people want if they are not able to do it by themselves or if the job they want to get done is more serious than just moving a few pieces around, if many changes are needed to be done or if the nature of the change is more complicated, for instance, changes like adding or removing walls and windows.

This is when you as an interior designer or decorator will receive a call. You can certainly help people professionally by following the space planning process.

A diagram which shows the stages of the process (flowchart) is given to show you a series of actions that you take in order to achieve the result.

Later, each of the titles will be discussed to make it crystal clear and to walk you through the process.

1—Predesign

    a—Observe

    b—Interview

    c—Identify

    d—Measure

2—Design

    a—Bubble Diagram

    b—Rough Sketches (Block plan)

3—Presentation

    a—Verbal

    b—Drawings   Plan

    (Put it on paper)   Elevation

                                   Section

                                   Perspective

                                 Detail

Home is a place to unwind, to be comfortable, and a place to show off the personal style. Everybody wants to create an oasis to relax, and we all are trying to find the right surroundings to help us to live or work in a more beautiful space with better conditions. People can have a varied range of their own personal styles, such as very sophisticated, bold, wild, mysterious, super modern, strange, pioneer . . . style, etc. (wrong or right, these are the words my clients or students used to describe their personal style.). Keep in mind that no matter what your client wants, the process of space planning and the method you use to achieve the target will stay the same; objects and physical qualities of those objects like color and form and the way you put those objects beside each other (arrangement style) will create what they want. You still should follow the flowchart to finish the job in a professional manner.

There are many different sources for each subject in this book. Despite the fact that there is a variation in technique, terminology, and the order of the tasks to be done, the reality is that they are not far from each other. Learning and working with the process provided here will make you able to understand the other existing variation in the field.

The attempt here is to pick what I, based on study, practice, and working with students, believe is efficient and easy to follow while the other techniques can be as sufficient as this one.

Back to the chart, we will start with the tasks that should be done in the predesign stage.

Predesign

a—Observe

A tour of the entire house or the portion you are supposed to work on is necessary.

Before even talking to the clients about their needs and wants, ask them to give you a tour around the house and explain it to them that you are not going to change anything without their permission and desire. This is just to see, understand, and feel what they already liked or had in their house. If they are not willing to have the walk—through, which sometimes happen, ask them for a tour around the room or the portion of the house that needs the changes.

Have your pen and paper ready to write down what you think is very important and pay attention to noticeable and not noticeable elements, such as architectural features like columns and pilasters, a very obvious dominant color, and existing decorative items, especially the big ones or a beautiful expensive handmade rug.

Do not assume and do not criticize. Just keep the notes for yourself to use them later.

b—Interview

A very important part of the process is verbal communication. The primary goal for the interview is to understand the client's needs and dreams (wants), musts and shoulds, his/her taste, style, and color scheme preference.

Sometimes people do not know what they really want or do not know how to explain it, therefore your questions will help them to organize their thought and their answers are a guideline in design process.

A very good listening ability is an asset. Proper, straight-to-the-point questions and questionnaires for collecting more detailed information will be very helpful.

This is a sample of questions you can ask about the family room:

1- Is this a place for the family itself or you are planning for parties?
2- What kind of feeling do you want to have? That of an elegant library or a homespun hangout?
3- Do kids play here? Or is it more for formal entertaining?
4- How much seating do you think you need?
5- Does the room need to work as a home office?
6- Does homework happen here?
7- Does any kind of art practicing like painting or playing instruments happen here?
8- Do you want to fit a big piece like a piano here?
9- Do you have enough outlets here?

Sure you can find many more questions just about the *function* of the room which certainly is the most important factor for the purpose of space planning.

If you are responsible for more than just the furniture arrangement, for instance, color scheme of the space, then you can have your questionnaires for the sake of color preferences. This is a page with different questions about colors. You can make your own sheet, or you can find predesigned ones in related books.

Here you can see some questions you can use in your questionnaires:

Question:

Don't think about any piece of cloth or furniture and react to the name of the color. Which one do you automatically prefer the best?

- Red
- Orange
- Yellow
- Green
- Blue
- Violet
- Black

Question:

How do you feel about these colors? Circle your choice.

Blue: sad, sleepy, lazy, calm, restful, peaceful

Yellow: aggravated, joyful, friendly, irritated, happy, hungry

Brown: dingy, bored, soothed, relaxed, calm

And continue with the other colors like green, gray, purple, white, orange, turquoise, and more. You can find many sources about color psychology even if you search online.

Question:

How do the existing colors in your room make you feel?

- Wall color is, _____ and it makes me feel _____.
- Sofa or chair color is, and it makes me feel _____.
- Floor color is, _____ and it makes me feel _____.

And continue with a few more features in the room. Do not overwhelm.

Question:

Think about your favorite room in your home and tell me which of the following moods you prefer to have in that room:

Name of the room: _____

- Bold and adventurous
- Ultramodern
- Surprising and unexpected
- Dainty and feminine
- Rugged and masculine
- Rich and opulent
- Soothing and tranquil
- Peaceful and calm
- Subdued
- Elegant

- Sophisticated
- Romantic
- Classic
- Welcoming and relaxing
- Edgy and modern
- Upbeat and happy

More than a few are mentioned here to make you familiar with the terms you can use in your verbal communication. You may also add to this list if you can think about any other mood you are able to create in one's space.

c—Identify

Based on your observation and interview, identify the rooms or areas which need to change. If you have any suggestion for your client about adjacent functional areas, it would be the best time to discuss. Make a list of areas and mention what are the needs and wants in these rooms. Your list should show the priorities, and this is very important, as in space planning, one rarely can find a solution to meet all the problems, but one should always start from the top of the list and try to find the best design solution for what is the most important issue for the client. Upon their approval, you can start measuring those spaces in order to proceed to design stage.

d—Measure

To build a house, the architect or the builder will submit an architectural plan to the City Hall with all the measurements. You should ask for the original plan if it is available, but not always can you find a useful, scaled, and accurate plan of the house or room that you want to work on, and that is why you need to measure the place to create your own plan with all the information you need for the space planning project.

You need a long enough steel measuring tape (at least twenty-five-foot long is recommended), a piece of paper, and a pencil to measure and draw a rough sketch of a room or an area. For beginners, grabbing a sheet of grid paper is recommended, otherwise any kind of paper can work.

Grid, graph, or millimeter paper, these are all different names for writing or drawing paper that is printed with fine lines, making up a regular grid.

To practice, pick a room in your house, for instance the bedroom, draw the overall shape of the room, and then start measuring the walls. Start from one corner and continue around the room until you reach to the same corner. Write down the measurements. Go back and measure all the openings and mark them in your drawing. Do not forget to measure from a corner to the window and then the width of the window, for this is how you can draw where the opening is located along the wall. Also, you can note down the height of the window to know if there is enough room to put different pieces of furniture without blocking the light or the view. For example, if you are working on a bedroom and you plan to put a high headboard attached to the bed, you would definitely want to know what the height of the window sill from the floor is.

Add all the architectural features like the fireplace, pillars, or pilasters, and just follow the shape of the outlines. Do not worry about the quality of lines, but be accurate in measuring. In this phase the rule is: "the more clean and tidy your draft, the easier to draw the scaled plan later." You should also mark all the electrical and mechanical outlets as they have a strong impact on your space planning. Note down the north side and the best view.

Now you are ready to draw a scaled plan to start working on your design.

Note: If you have the ability to draw and have some experience in this field, it is obvious that you can continue with this chapter; if not, you may want to go to the chapter "basics of drafting" to know about the tools and techniques to make sure that you know how to draw a scaled plan. Later you can come back to this chapter to continue with different steps of space planning process.

Design

a—Bubble diagram

This is a relationship diagram to show roughly "what goes where" and also is to draw to make you able to check the traffic flow or the traffic pattern in that space.

It is a trial-and-error method to explore all the planning options, so the planner or other viewers should not jump to a conclusion, judgment, or critic.

Read and analyze the collected information in the predesign stage and make a list of priorities; in other words, have a list of:

- must haves
- would be nice to have

- not important at all

It takes a very skilled professional to create the best design in the first attempt. For more complicated, big commercial projects even professionals need to examine a few alternatives to solve the problem or to find the best design option.

A bubble diagram would be very helpful in this stage and should be thought as a first step of design for all types and sizes of interior spaces.

Tape the scaled floor plan you created to the drafting board and put a piece of tracing paper on top; any kind of markers or pencils can help but the best is a very soft pencil which moves easily to create a bold mark without that much effort. Draw a circle for each function considering the relationship between the functions.

Check the traffic pattern by drawing arrows in the same direction as the traffic flow.

It is a good idea to record thoughts about special factors while doing the bubble diagram as well as recording the positive and negative points of each combination.

In the next page you can see how to use the bubble diagram technique to start a design process for a master bedroom suite with adjacent walking closet(s) and bathroom.

You can also use the bubble diagram method to arrange the furniture in one single space. The traffic flow, where entering and leaving the room and between furniture should be examined.

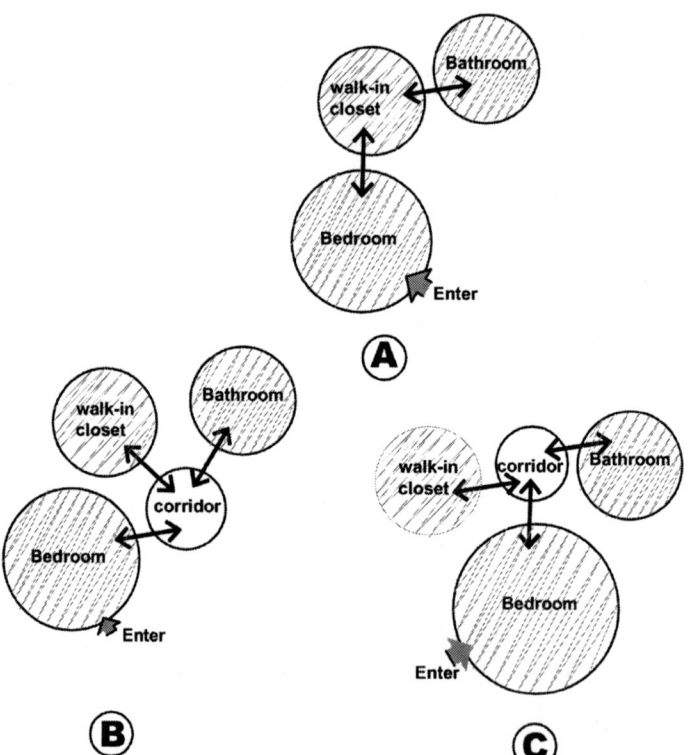

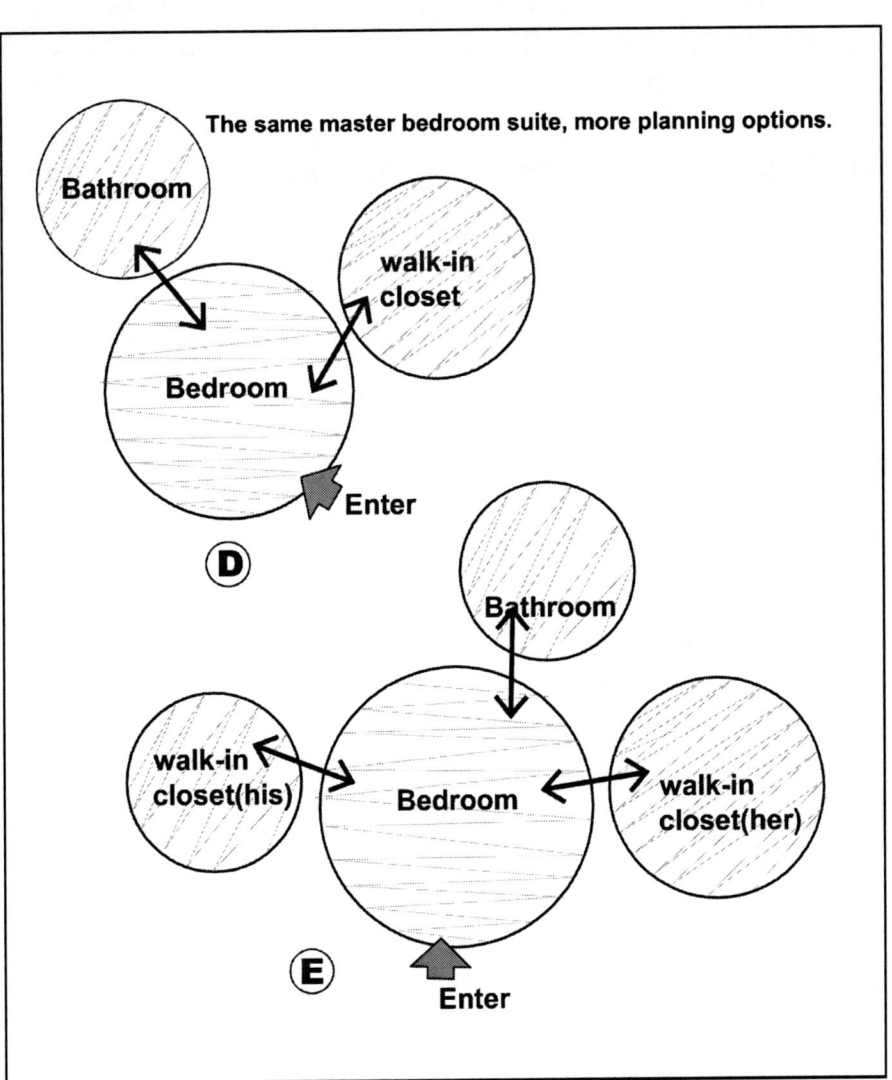

b—Rough sketch (Block plan)

Review all the options created in bubble diagrams, talk to your client or colleagues, and consider the advantages/disadvantages of each option until you are comfortable with one or two of them.

For these, one or two preferred options, you should define different spaces by drawing rough but almost scaled rectangular blocks which will fill the plan's outline.

A scaled empty plan is needed to add the designed interior items which still are not very neat and detailed to show the final decisions. You can create this or these plans by drawing the outline of furniture and any architectural elements you want to build in this place, for example, a counter, pony wall, or fireplace.

This plan should include windows and doors and the approximate place of existing electrical outlets to show that it is possible to connect the lamps, TV, computer as needed, otherwise you need to consult with an electrician to change the location of the outlets or any other lighting fixture.

You can discuss this plan or these plans, if you have more than one option, with your client. Restrict the options to a maximum of three as it would be very confusing for nonprofessional people to pick one.

In this stage also you can add a rough sketch of elevation, section, and perspective drawing to show all your ideas and the spatial considerations.

You and your client should reach to an agreement about one of the possibilities, and then you can proceed to a final presentation to get the final approval. Ask your client to sign the selected option.

Presentation

When all the influential issues like budget and the overall style are discussed, the functions are identified, the relation between functional spaces are approved, and the best option suggested by the designer is recognized and signed by the client, then it is the showtime. It is the time to show the final product of the space planning project. Every step of the space planning process is of great significance for achieving the professional result; likewise, the presentation requires enough attention to details, and it can happen verbally or by the help of drawings.

a—Verbal

Verbal communication is one way for people to communicate face-to-face. Sounds and words are some of the verbal communication's main component but keep in mind that words alone have no meaning and only people can put meaning into work.

When you are going to represent your design in school or in front of your clients, to be clear, professional, positive, and enthusiastic is the best approach for a successful verbal presentation and the best way to convey the design ideas.

Jargons are special words in professional fields, and each field has its own jargon words. Particularly with clients, using jargons slightly sounds professional, while too much of jargons will confuse your client. You don't want to put them down by showing off your knowledge, but you want to convince them that your design suits their needs and desires and is a reflection of their personal style.

Do you think it sounds great if you say, "You need to add a *transom* on top of the door and should put two *klismos* chair on each side, and you also need a *jabot* for your window treatment"?

In an actual verbal presentation, you should explain each of your suggestions clearly; at the end, you may inform your client that in the professional world we call them by different words.

Thus you should say, "To bring enough light in this room, it's better to add a window on top of the door, which is called *transom*. Having two chairs in *ancient Greek style* will help us to create the kind of traditional style you liked to see in this room. I am going to look around to find two *Klismos* chairs for you. In addition, we will change the look of your drape to a more dramatic look by adding long, pleated pieces to the end of each side, as you might know they are called *jabot*."

It would be a wonderful idea to have a few pictures from magazines or the Internet to make it clear how the items look like when talking about them.

When the space planning problem is relatively easy to solve, verbal presentation may work without supporting documents or drawings, but most of the time drawings are needed to describe the new ideas and changes.

b—Drawings

The end product of space planning is a good quality drawing of floor plan, and if there is any need for more clarification, we need to draw elevations, sections, and perspective. These drawings explain the other aspects of design. For instance, an elevation shows the height of the room and the other objects in that room, while plan is able to show the width and the length of the room and everything inside it. Preparing a sample board at the earlier stage of a project to convey the design concept is an additional attempt to study real samples of materials before any final decision is made.

Chapter 2

Drafting

Basics of Drafting

(Put it on paper)

It is possible to draft and draw the design ideas by using computer. With the help of a drawing software like Auto Cad, Archie Cad, carol and . . . you will be able to draft your ideas, develop them, and to create your presentation drawings like plans, elevations, sections, details, and even perspectives, but the main purpose of this chapter is to show you how to represent an efficient space plan even without computer work, which I believe is a necessary tool for more complicated projects. Later, if you are master of both, good for you, you can decide how to use the combination of both skills to impress your clients.

When planning to create a functional and charming space or to change the existing selection and style for better, most probably plan is the only required drawing for the smaller, less complicated projects, but in bigger projects with more spatial consideration, a set of drawing is needed.

A set of drawing usually includes: floor plans, elevations, sections, layouts, and often details and perspective. You may also need mechanical and electrical plans.

These drawings will create more clarification for your design and is a facilitator to convey that idea to your client. Besides, contractors and subcontractors need those drawings to know what you need and where you need it.

Floor Plan

Plan is a horizontal section of a building, four feet above the floor.

For beginners or nonprofessionals, it is the first difficult part to absorb, but it is easy to understand if you imagine you are cutting a tomato parallel to the countertop with a knife. What if you have a very big knife with a long and wide blade to cut a room or a building four feet above the floor?

Cut the tomato and put the top part aside and look at the other part from the above. Pay attention to what you can see.

Now imagine what you will see if you cut through an empty room with one window on one side and a door on the other side. Later in this chapter, you will see the plan of this room.

From all drawings in a set of drawing, floor plan is the most important one, and it is the first to be created and developed. To draw the other drawings, like elevations or sections, you need to have a precise floor plan or plans if the building has more than one story or level.

In an architectural floor plan, you can see:

- the external walls, their thickness and length
- position of the rooms
- size of the rooms
- position, dimension, and operation direction of all openings
- location and size (width and length) of the architectural and interior features (columns, fireplace, stairs . . .)
- location and size (width and length) of major appliances
- outside features (patio, deck, balcony, poles)
- material symbols
- title block which is to show name of the company or designer, name of the drawing, scale of the drawing, and more)
- scale of the drawing is to clarify the proportion of the actual sizes to the dimension shown in drawings (how much smaller is the drawing compared to reality); it can be part of the title block or written below the drawing. The scale most commonly used for space planning is 1/4" = 1' − 0"
- the position of the building toward four main directions: north, south, east, and west

Rules, symbols, and standards will be the same regardless of complication or size of the construction. In bigger and more complicated projects, more details are needed, but drawing essentials remain the same.

Elevation

Stand in front of a wall and look straight. Imagine everything you see is on a flat vertical surface; the image is the elevation of that wall. Elevations are the straight-on views of vertical surfaces,; they have no depth, and all the curved or diagonal surfaces are projected onto the flat plane of the drawing. The height of the exterior walls, windows, doors, and architectural features are shown in the elevation.

In interior design, elevations will show the wall from inside the room and the furniture on or close to that wall. Each room usually has four wall elevation or even more if the shape of the room is not just a square.

Section

Take your imaginary knife, put it anywhere on the roof of the building, and cut straight through it from top to bottom, separate one piece and position in front of the other part. What you can see is the section of the building. You can have as many sections as needed to show all the necessary details, again no depth and all on a flat surface of your drawing paper.

Perspective

Perspective is a three-dimensional drawing to show the spatial ideas. Every object in perspective has the correct size and position in comparison with other things in the drawing.

In next page you will see a rectangular room with a door and a window. The elevation, section, and the perspective of the room in the same page will give you a better idea about the drawings and the details they can add to our perception from the room. After that you can see an architectural main floor plan of a modern residential building.

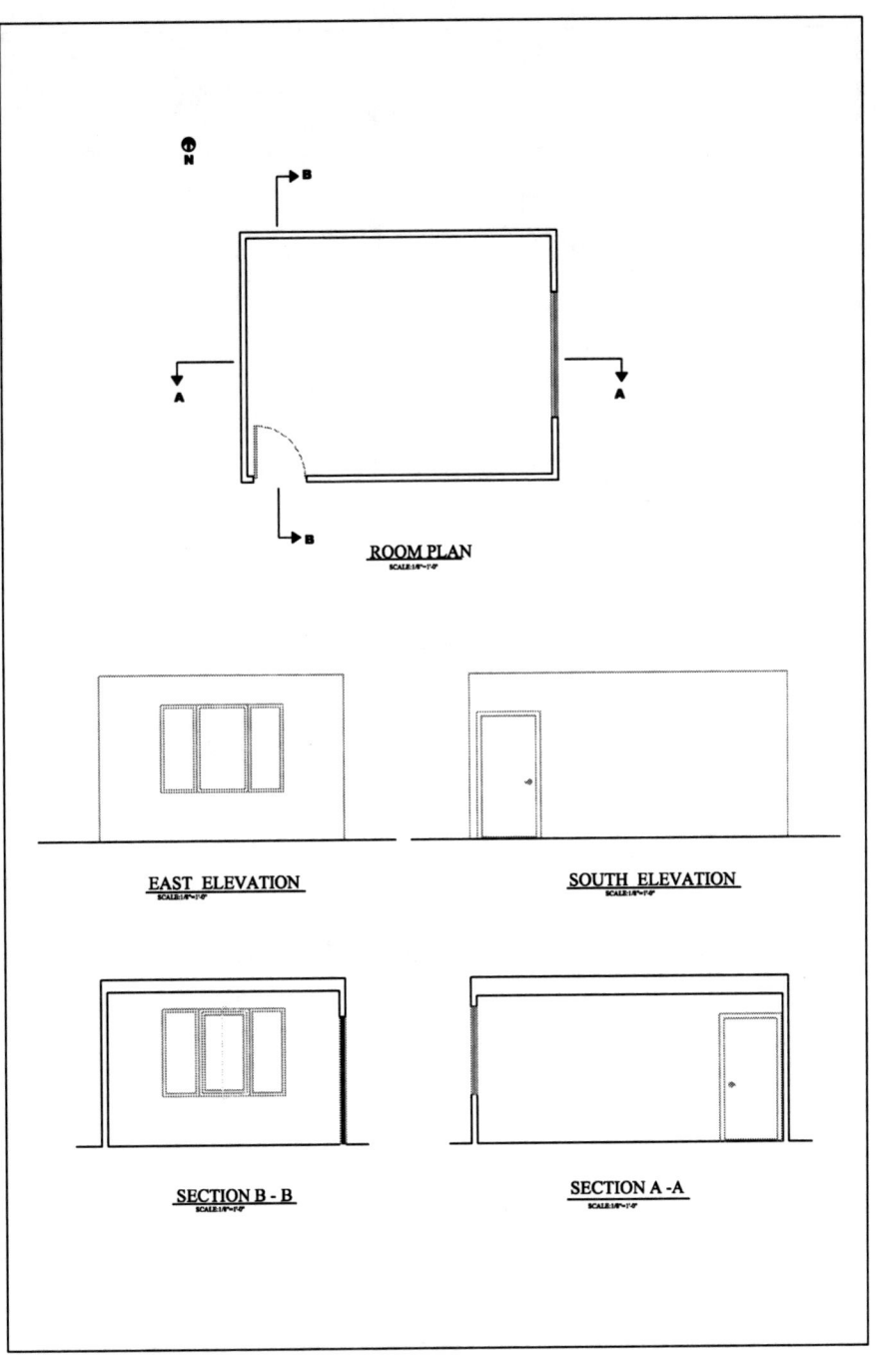

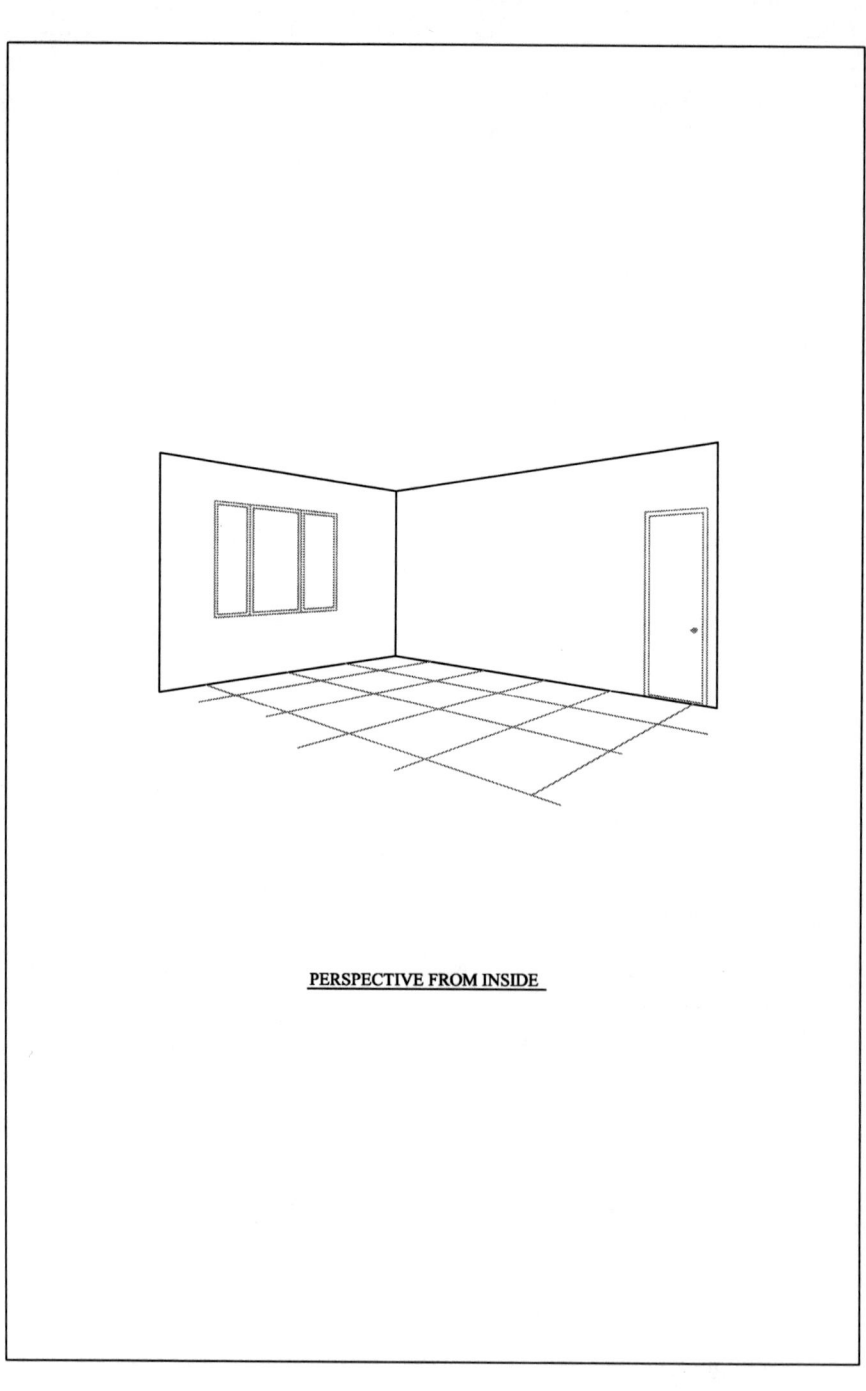

PERSPECTIVE FROM INSIDE

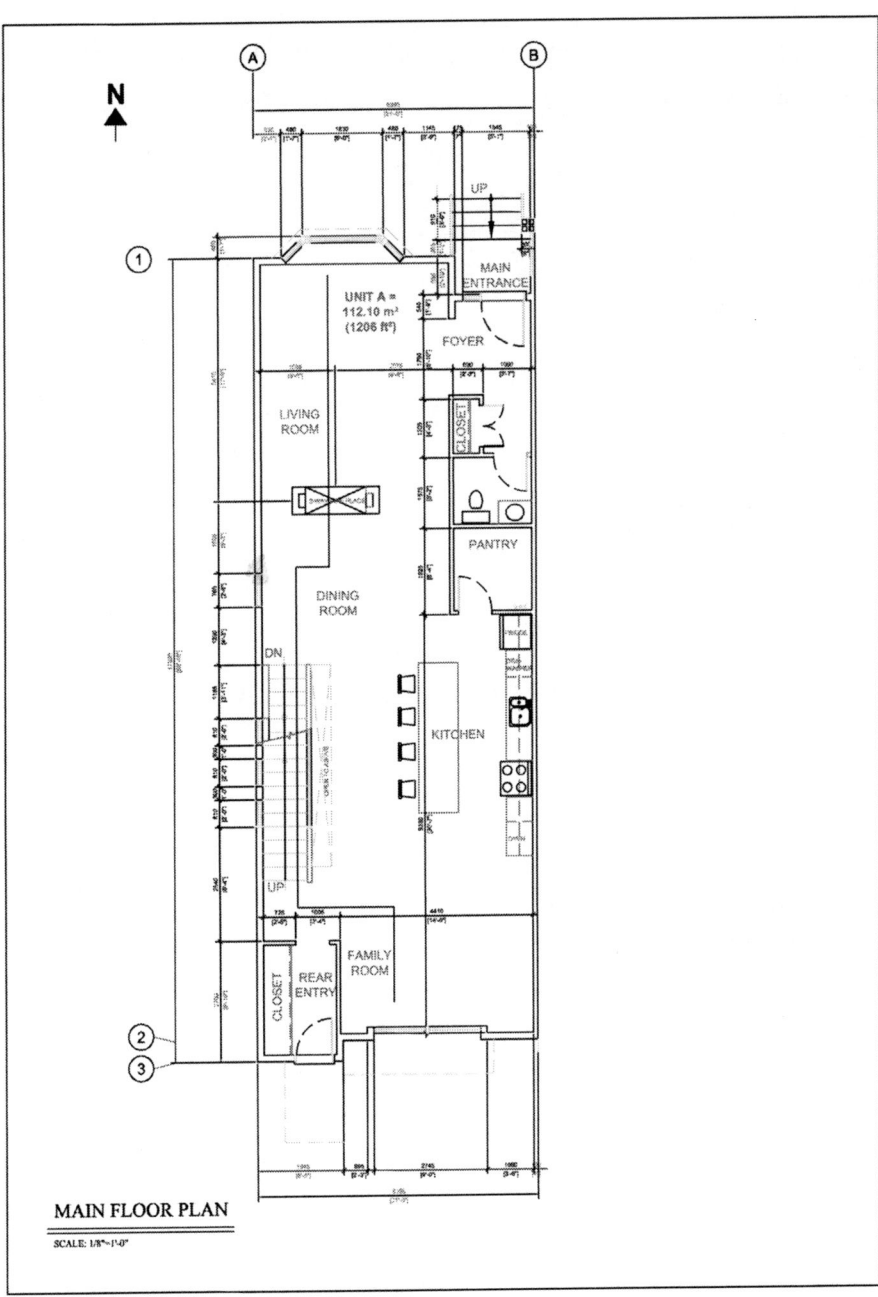

MAIN FLOOR PLAN
SCALE: 1/8"=1'-0"

Drawing Tools

To start even a very simple hand-drawing plan (not computer drawing) for the purpose of space planning, some tools are needed:

- Drawing board or table
- Paper
- T-ruler
- Scale
- Triangle
- Pencils
- Eraser
- Erasing guide
- Sharpener
- Template
- Masking tape
- There are also a few more tools that you may or may not need:
- Protractor
- Curves

Art supply stores usually have these items in a drafting set, drawing kit, or as a single item to buy. There are many Web sites which sell these items online.

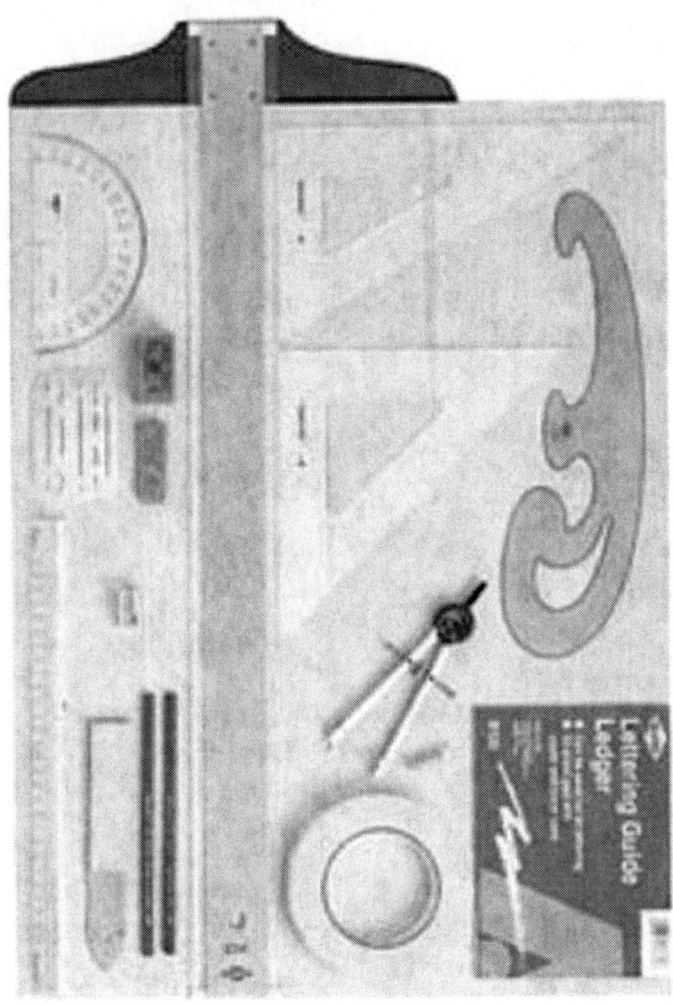

In this kit you can see almost everything you need to start.

Drawing board and table

Drawing boards are made of plastic or wood and come in few different sizes. A plastic board 30"x20"or even a small wooden board 13"x10" is usually enough for home works and small jobs.

Some of the boards have a ruler attached to them, and for some, you need to use your T-ruler.

Drawing, drafting, or architectural desk is a kind of multipurpose desk which can be used for any kind of drawing, writing, or sketching on a large sheet of paper.

Drawing table   drawing board with attached ruler

Paper

Graph paper, tracing paper, and vellum are the most common papers used for space planning.

Grid, graph, graphing, or millimeter paper are all different names for writing or drawing paper that is printed with fine lines, making up a regular grid. The lines are often used as guides for hand-drawing plans, and each square's side represents one foot to create a scaled drawing of ¼" = 1' – 0". Later in this chapter we will talk about scale ruler.

Tracing paper is thin enough to be see-through (transparent) and is the best for sketching.

Pencils with different thicknesses are the most proper tool to draw on tracing paper. You can buy them in rolls which is good for sketching and sheet which is easier to use and comes in different sizes.

Vellum is a kind of heavier, higher quality, more durable paper and is also transparent but thicker than tracing paper. Vellum is made mostly for ink drawing and is available both in rolls and sheets.

T-ruler or T square

T square looks like the letter T. Top of the T square is vertical, and the long part is horizontal. In order to use the T square correctly you need to tape your paper to a drawing board, making sure that the edges of the paper are parallel to the edges of the drawing board. Then, by sliding the T square along the side of the drawing board, you can draw parallel lines. To make a paper's edge parallel to the drawing board's edge, you can also use your T-ruler without taping the paper down. Just use your hand to adjust your paper parallel to the ruler and then tape it down. The T-ruler edge is always parallel to the edge of the drawing board.

Scale

It is not possible to draw a house plan or even a room's plan with the actual dimensions they have in real world, but it is possible to draw them in reduced scale.

An architect's scale is a specialized ruler. It is used for scaled drawing and is available in imperial and metric system.

You can find a wooden scale or scale made of aluminum, but what is mostly used by architects and interior designers is made of plastic and usually has a triangle section.

Take the scale and turn it a few times to see the ratios written at both end of the scale. In imperial scale you will see ratios like, 1/2, 1/4, 1/8, 3/4, 3/8, 3/16, 3/32.

Scale 1/2 means 1/2" in drawing is equal to 1' – 0" in the real world, and it is the same for the other ratios as well, for example, scale 1/8 (one eight) means 1/8 inch in drawing is the equivalent of one foot and zero inch in reality (1/8" = 1' – 0").

Until the 1970s, Canada traditionally used the imperial system of measurement units and then converted to metric system.

In metric regular flat rulers, the smallest measuring unit is millimeter,

centimeter (cm) = 10 millimeter (mm)

meter (m) = 100 cm

while in imperial system, the smallest unit on regular rulers is 1/8 inch and in some 1/16 inch.

1' (1foot) = 12" (inches)

1 yard = 3 foot

Although in Canada, the official system is metric, trades are more familiar with imperial measuring units. In interior space planning projects, a commonly used scale is 1/4" = 1' – 0".

On metric scale there are ratios like 1:10, 1:20, 1:25, 1:50, 1:75, 1:100, 1:125, 1:200, 1:500, 1:750, 1:1000.

When you want to buy a scale, it is important to know that each scale has six different ratios. In interior space planning, you should pick the scale which has one to ten, one to twenty, one to twenty-five, and one to fifty, as the space planning projects mostly are drawn in scale = 1:50.

Scale 1/4" = 1' – 0" in imperial system is equal to 1/48 in metric system.

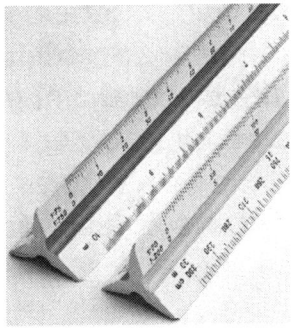

Triangle

Triangle is usually made of transparent plastic and is to draw horizontal, vertical, and angled lines. The 45, 45, 90 degree triangle and 30, 60, 90 degree triangles are available in different sizes and colors.

Put your T square ruler on your drawing board; you will be able to draw a horizontal line. Take a triangle and put it on top of the T-ruler while one of the sides is attached to the ruler; now you will be able to draw a vertical line. Try to see that by moving the triangle without moving the ruler, you can draw multiple vertical lines.

30, 60, 90degree triangle   45, 45, 90degree

Pencil

Drawing pencils are defined by letters and numbers 6B, 4B, 2B, HB, 2H or 4H pencil is how we recognize them. B series are softer than H series. The bigger the number in B pencils, the softer the lead of the pencil is. Do not use very soft pencils like 6B or 4B to draw the final plan as they will cause your drawing to smudge. These soft leads are perfect for bubble diagram and rough sketches.

Not like B series of pencils, the less the number in H leads, the softer the pencil is. HB, 2H, and 4H pencils are good to create the set of drawing. 4H is the hardest one and one should be careful not to cut the tracing paper by putting lots of hand pressure when working with a 4h pencil.

Eraser

White erasers are softer and clean the drawing better than the other kinds available in the market.

Erasing guide

This is a metal, thin sheet with some holes in different shapes on it and is to help you clean tiny part of your drawing by revealing the small part which needs to be clean and covering the other parts.

Sharpener

Sharp, pointed leads are needed to create a quality drawing which is professional and clean. There is a variety of sharpeners you can use to sharpen your pencil. A good quality metal one with sharp blades is very efficient but will leave that curvy mess behind.

One of the easiest manual pencil sharpeners to use that most school rooms have (or had) is the one mounted at kid level—a fairly inexpensive and practical investment if you draw a lot.

Also you can find a newer version which works by turning the pencil instead of turning the handle, and both have a filter to clean the lead from the black powder after sharpening the lead. Use the sharpener and the filter regularly to draw clean lines.

Template

Furniture templates and templates for drawing circles are available in different shapes and scales.

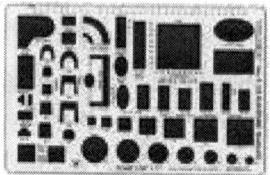   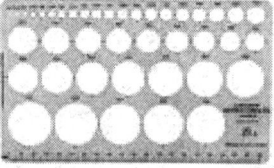

Furniture template   Circle template

A good quality scale 1/4" = 1' – 0" furniture template is necessary in space planning to draw furniture as well as to make your own cutouts.

A template with circles in different sizes will help you to draw the footstep of a door swing and many more curves and circles that you need to show in your plan.

Protractor

It is a drawing tool to precisely measure and to draw different angles. A protractor is marked from 0 to 180 degree.

Masking tape

When you draw on a table or board, the paper needs to be fixed by a masking tape. In the drafting kit shown on page 45, you can see a ring of masking tape.

It is strong enough to keep the paper in place and is easy to remove without damaging the paper. But be careful not to tear the paper when you want to take it off.

Start to draw

Lines are fundamentals of drawing. Straight, horizontal, and vertical lines, as well as angled and curved lines are joined together to shape a drawing.

A quality drawing depends on the crispness of the lines.

Lines

Pencils	Line weight	Application
2B, 4B, 6B	Very Thick	Border line/Section line
HB	Thick	Sketch/Exterior and Interior Walls
H	Medium	Lettering/Furniture outline/Electrical, Lighting symbols
2H	Thin	Door and Window/ Dimension/Hidden line/ Centerline/Break Line/ Moving part/Leader/ Lettering
4H	Very Thin	Guide line

You can pick the pencil that is suitable for you even if it is not exactly what you can see in the table as some brands offer softer leads when compared to the others, and the hand pressure people put on the pencils are also different.

But the order should be the same; for example, if you use H instead of HB to draw the walls, then for furniture outline you can use 2H and for doors and windows 4H will be an option.

All lines, thick, medium or thin, have a few things in common:

- Lines must have a definite beginning and end.

- Line should be even with the same thickness from the start point to the end. Keep your hand pressure even and slowly rotate your pencil.
- All lines should be crisp and sharp, not soft and fuzzy; in this case sharpen and wipe the lead.

Never use the scale to draw a line, for a **scale is not a ruler** and is made to measure. T-ruler and triangle are the tools you should use when working on a drawing board or table. Use a regular ruler or triangle to draw on grid paper.

Now that you know what a plan is and are familiar with drawing tools, line weight, and line quality, you can start practicing and working with your tools to obtain some experience to draw lines with different thicknesses and lines in different scales. Later you will be able to draw a room plan and ultimately a house plan.

Assignment no. 1: Line weight

- Draw a vertical guide line
- Draw 5 very thin horizontal guide lines, spaced ¼" apart
- Starting at the vertical guide line, measure 5" and mark five lines
- Draw and identify the line weights as follows:

    1. Very thick
    2. Thick
    3. Medium
    4. Thin
    5. Very thin

-A guide line is a very thin and pale line just to mark the start point and the direction of the lines in this assignment.

In general, as the name offers, it is a thin line to guide you whenever it is needed, and after finishing the drawing, it should be erased without leaving a mess behind. Use a very hard lead like 4H and draw the guide line with minimum hand pressure.

If the paper you use is a grid, graph paper, you don't need the guide line. It is a good habit to leave at least one inch from each side of the paper as a margin. Pick a vertical line far left on the paper, but after the margin, and start working on horizontal lines which already exist ¼" apart.

You may choose tracing paper, vellum, yellow draft paper, or a regular white letter size (A4) paper; in this case you need to use your T-ruler and triangle to draw the vertical guide line then mark the vertical line ¼" apart. Use the T-ruler to draw the horizontal lines by supporting the head of the ruler with your left hand and moving it to the marks. When using a T-ruler, always make sure that the head is attached to the board otherwise the lines turn to be oblique and not horizontal.

- Border lines are drawn to create a border for the drawing and will leave a margin of 1" to 1 1/2" around the paper sheet.

- The paper size commonly used in residential space planning is 8 1/2" × 11"; for the purpose of project no. 1 and no. 2, you can use grid paper in the same size.

Assignment no. 2: Use of scale

- Starting the vertical guide line, draw four very thin horizontal guide lines, 1/4" apart.
- Use your scale to measure and mark following distances:

    1. Scale 1/8" = 1' – 0"   length = 24' – 6"
    2. Scale 1/4" = 1' – 0"   length = 12' – 9"
    3. Scale 1/4" = 1' – 0"   length = 7' – 7"
    4. Scale 3/4" = 1' – 0"   length = 4' – 2"

- Draw the appropriate line lengths in medium weight and print the length and scale next to each line, as shown above.
- Draw the border line with 1½" gap from the paper outline.

Scale 1/8 and 1/4 are both on one line, and each starts from 0 on different end of your scale; before number 0, it shows one foot which is divided to 12 inches. Use this part to measure inches after you measured foots for your assignment.

Now that you practiced to draw lines with different thicknesses and to use your scale ruler to measure and draw lines, we assume that you are ready to go back to the "Residential interior space planning" to continue with design step.

Start to Draw a Furniture Plan

Start to work on a single room in your own home, for example, your bedroom, which most probably has one or more doors and at least one window. Later, by obtaining more knowledge and by more practice, you can work on a house plan or even more complicated projects.

Use your sketch drawing created during the measuring step of the predesign process to draw the scaled plan. Tape the paper on drawing board, use your T ruler to draw horizontal lines, your scale ruler to measure lines in scale 1/4"=1'-0" and triangle to draw vertical or angular lines. you can add the thickness of the walls by drawing outside lines parallel to the internall walls with 4"-6" gap in between, do not forget the openings. This would be your 1/4"=1'-0" scaled plan.

Look closely and measure the bed, side table, lamp, and everything you have in your bedroom, also the distance between those items. Tape down your ¼" = 1' – 0" scaled plan; using your furniture template try to draw the outline of your bedroom furniture. If the size of the cutouts are not exactly the same as the furniture in the room, use your T-ruler and triangle and adjust the size of them by your vertical and horizontal lines. It is a good practice to get involved without the pressure of creating a new design. Now that you practiced a little bit with your tools and have the existing plan in your hand, pretend that you need a new arrangement in this room. Space planning design steps should be followed line by line.

See if you want to remove some of the items, want to add something, or just want to rearrange the existing furniture. Use the bubble diagram technique to create a few options and to check the traffic patterns. Pick the best and use the template or the cutouts provided in the "Room by Room" chapter to draw the new design.

Here you can see a living and dining room which needed a new arrangement as well as the new design which shows a small but effective change.

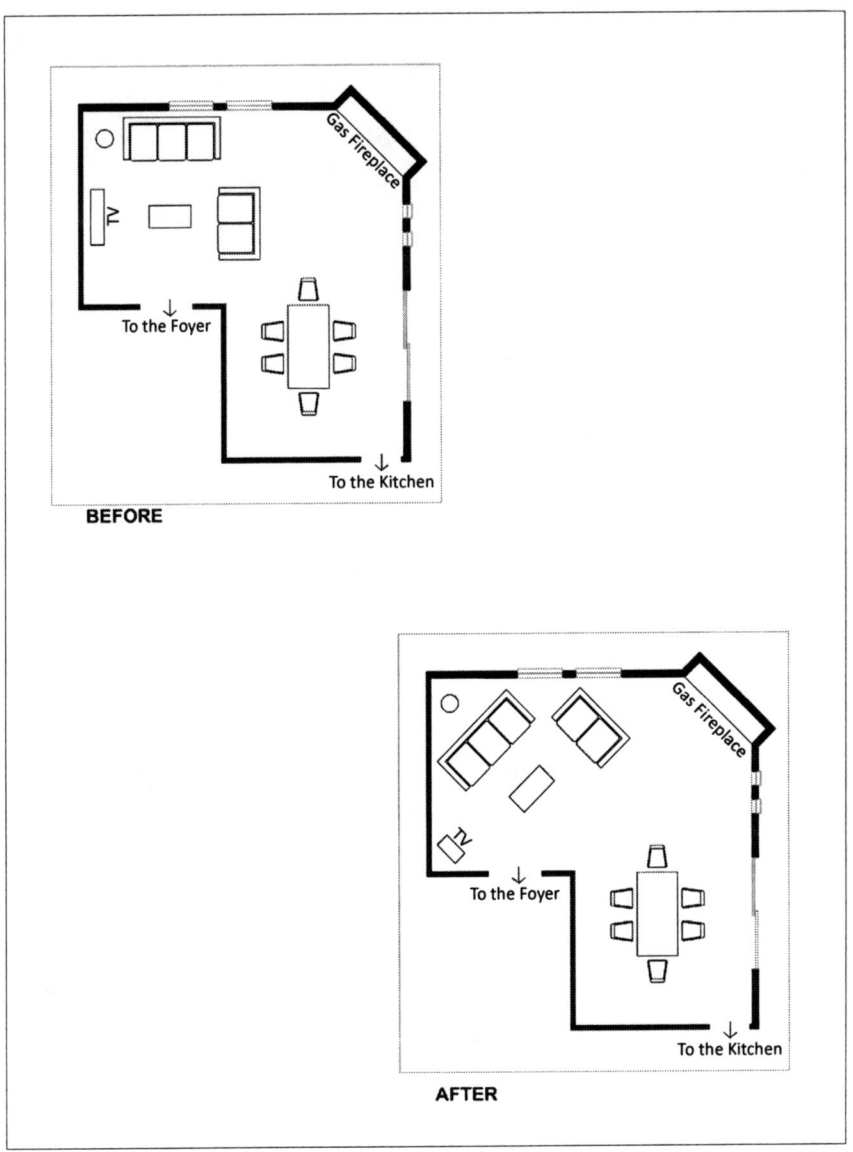

Chapter 3

Accessible and Green Design

Accessible and Green

Some titles should be studied as they are closely related to space planning.

Upon entering the world of design, you frequently will hear terms like barrier-free design, accessible design, or universal design.

You also may hear terms like green design, eco-friendly design, environmentally friendly design, or sustainable design which are highly discussed these days.

Pages and pages of information are available in books, magazines and Web sites which discuss these subjects from different point of views, but here we will put them in two categories "Barrier-Free Design" and "Green Design" and will try to explain the basic meaning and usage of them.

There are different courses offered by universities and colleges about green design or sustainability. You also may study part 3 of Canadian "National Building Code" and guide to barrier-free design to find more about accessible or universal design and spatial consideration which can create an accessible building.

Finally, if you are interested in more detailed information, you can find many books and magazines about both subjects in your local library which is easy to access with almost no cost.

Green Design

Designing high-performance buildings with least or if possible no environmental impact and providing highest level of comfort for occupants is discussed under different titles like green design, environmentally friendly design, sustainable design, or holistic design.

It is still an open end subject on which scientists, economists, producers, and designers are working so much so that new products are being introduced to the market almost every day.

As far as interior designers and space planners are concerned, designing interiors that care for the health and well-being of people and the natural environment is what we mean when discussing green design.

Effective project management, regardless of the size of the project, is to *reduce* the amount of waste we produce, and it applies to even small family projects.

Whenever possible, *reuse* an item or find someone who can use it.

You commit yourself to a green action to protect the natural resources when you repair and renew an old item to use it again and again. When donating old items to organizations in need, you are creating the opportunity for somebody else to reuse and to save the nature.

Our valuable natural resources can be protected if *recycling* is a habit, as in the recycling process, we reuse the already made material to make something new instead of cutting or excavating more natural resources.

"Reduce, Reuse, and Recycle" are the three famous Rs to learn about in green design.

However designing with materials which are easy to reproduce is another way to be part of this new responsibility. Products made of bamboo can be a good sample. Bamboo is the fastest-growing plant on earth and can be replaced easily when cut to make things like wood flooring.

Bamboo flooring has a natural, charming look and is water resistant thus suitable to be used everywhere, even in the kitchen.

There are many more you can do as a responsible space planner when designing different rooms and spaces in a house; for instance, a simple square you draw in a kitchen floor plan to show the location of the refrigerator has a lot to say about green design. The size of the square will show how big the fridge is, and most probably your client needs your idea to choose his or her new fridge.

Convince your client not to go for fridges with ice maker as they use more energy than the one with ice racks; teach them that they can use smaller size fridges which is more energy efficient than the larger options, also the fact that bottom-freezer models are generally the most energy-efficient models.

Make them familiar with the energy star label; they will use this knowledge to pick the other green product as well.

Suggesting and implementing these ideas result in a greener design which is good for the environment as well as for the client's health while it can save lots of money for them when they pay lesser for the consumed energy each month.

Other energy-saving devices that can be used in homes are as follows:

- Low flash toilets which are water-saving toilets only use between one and two gallons of water per flush compared to the usual three to five gallons.
- Renewable flooring such as bamboo and cork flooring as well as natural linoleum are considered green products. Cork comes from the bark of a tree that can be harvested once every ten years, and bamboo comes from an Asian grass; it matures in about six years. Cork reduces the noise and is a thermal insulator. Bamboo has the same hardness

as other wood flooring, a very natural look, and is more resistant against water.
- LED lighting or "light-emitting diode" is an environmentally friendly light that gives off the same light as a regular 40-watt bulb, but lasts fifty times longer. LED light bulbs present many advantages over incandescent light sources, including lower energy consumption, longer lifetime, smaller size, faster switching, and greater durability and reliability which make the product a very cost-effective option to light the home. Bellow is the comparison chart between LED, compact fluorescent, and incandescent lighting bulbs, taken from "earth easy solution for sustainable living" Web site. (www.eartheasy.com)

	LED	CFL	Incandescent
Light bulb projected lifespan	50,000 hours	10,000 hours	1200 hours
Watts per bulb (equiv. 60 watts)	6	14	60
Cost per bulb	$35.95	$3.95	$1.25
KWh of electricity used over 50,000 hours	300	700	3000
Cost of electricity (@ 0.20per KWh)	$60	$140	$600
Bulbs needed for 50k hours of use	1	5	42
Equivalent 50k hours bulb expense	$35.95	$19.75	$52.50
Total cost for 50k hours	$95.95	$159.75	$652.50

- Not so long ago, it was common for fumes to drive people from their homes during the stage of painting when renovating their house or just when repainting their walls, as conventional paints contain high level of VOC (volatile organic compounds) that produce a breathable gas when applied; the off-gassing procedure will diminish air quality and is harmful to people's health. Today, alternative manufacturing techniques have allowed the development of low and no VOC paints that release no or minimal VOC pollutants and are odor free.
- Paint is one of the most powerful tools when changing the appearance of a home interior, as an owner or a designer always looks for low-VOC or no-VOC interior paint and in the same time keep in mind that paint is not the only product that can emit VOC or the other harmful chemicals, carpet and adhesives used in carpeting can be another product not good for the quality of indoor air and eventually not good for the health of humans. Your green carpeting options are carpets made of natural fibers like cotton, wool, or sea grass which are less likely to emit high level of VOCs and are made from renewable resources.
- Earthy, organic upholstery and window-treatment fabrics are options now to create greener homes.

Green design is internationally respected and can be certified by a system called Leed.

LEED (Leadership in Energy and Environmental Design) is an internationally recognized green building certification system, providing verification that a building or community was designed and built using strategies intended to improve performance in metrics such as energy savings, water efficiency, CO_2 emissions reduction, improved indoor environmental quality, and stewardship of resources and sensitivity to their impacts.

Developed by the *U.S. Green Building Council* (USGBC), **LEED** is intended to provide building owners and operators a concise framework for identifying and implementing practical and measurable green building design, construction, operations and maintenance solutions.

When you are hired as space planner to redesign a residential building, Leed can give you many options for a green design. Green design is not mandatory by law but is a fast-growing trend and a responsibility for all of us. The more you know about it, the more you want to apply it.

Barrier-Free Design

Having an overall view and a better understanding of the subject is necessary for everybody who is involved with the field of design. This part is not a guide to design accessible buildings.

To plan a new building, especially if it is a public facility, you need to study and practice to be able to design the building effectively, and it is a job for architects, but even planning typical, small residential spaces to make them accessible for different types of disabilities is a crucial matter that needs special attention to details. Until you gain more experience, consultation with specialists is always recommended. For more information and detailed guidance, you should check your local "building code" and the guide for barrier-free design.

"Safety Code Council" usually provides this guide based on latest building codes of the same country or province. These guides are focused on barrier-free design and are easier to follow as most of the rules are followed by detailed sketches and drawings that will clarify the true meaning and application of the rules.

What we are trying to do here is to discuss the concept of barrier-free design, which you, as a designer, should be familiar with and to help you to know where to go for more detailed information.

To define what "Barrier-Free Design" means, a couple of clear and meaningful definitions which almost cover all aspects of the subject are chosen here.

- Design for "independence and dignity for everyone" is the target of barrier-free design.
- The concept of universal design is to allow a built environment with its ability to adapt and to accommodate the needs of any user of the space including people with vision, hearing, communication, mobility and cognition disabilities.

These definitions are taken from Alberta building code and guide for barrier-free design 2008 by Alberta safety code council based on Alberta building code 2006, which do exist to allow proper and safe access to buildings and facilities and talks about spatial requirements, dimensions, signage, and many more details to consider when designing public facilities.

Based on these codes, single-family dwellings, houses including semi-detached houses, duplexes, triplexes, town houses, row houses, and boarding houses which are not used in social programs (group homes, halfway houses, and shelters) are *exempt* from barrier-free requirements.

It means that residential space planning which is the title of this book are under no obligation to execute those rules and codes, but at the same time, it is possible for a designer to be asked to renovate or redesign a home to be comfortable and safe to use for elderly or residents on wheelchair.

Design for the other disabilities or impairments except limited movement ability are not discussed here and are more involved with proper signage or device.

Residential space planning projects are impacted by limited movement ability, from minor (aging process) to major (wheelchair-bound) more than by the other problems.

In 1998, when attending a "Barrier-Free Design" seminar and workshop in Bangkok, Thailand, they made us spend half a day in wheelchairs while visiting a site that was a potential user of our design. This action had a very strong impact on me as well as on the other participants.

One year later I was invited by faculty of environment in University of Tehran to talk about the experience in Bangkok. Also, a few months later, I was assigned to teach a group of young boys to make them able to work with a team of designers who were supposed to make the city parks barrier free and possible to use for everybody, including people on wheelchairs. It was my turn to ask them one by one to sit in a wheelchair, pass through the door, and go to the bathroom to experience how frustrating it might be to want to be independent while bound to a wheelchair if the building is not proper to use.

It is a very interesting experience if you like to try; wheelchairs are everywhere in hospitals, retirement communities, or even in a friend's house. Try to get to the building to see the importance of a ramp or pass a door which is smaller than 800 mm or use the bathroom to see why you should have enough room to maneuver with wheelchair.

A barrier-free design is dimensionally demanding and needs a bigger space to be executed, otherwise we could remove all the barriers even in single-family houses or apartments to create a friendlier environment for all the users.

Rich dimension of chair-bound people

In housing for chair-bound people, controls for fixtures such as light switches, socket outlets, heaters, meters, and window openers should be within the comfortable reach of a person seated in a wheelchair.

The comfortable reach dimensions are different for men, women, and children. Human body and its joints have a great range of movement ability, greater than the comfortable reach, but still designers should work with static body position dimensions as it will work for the other positions like vertical, oblique, or oblique forward reach.

The area within comfortable reach is affected by the height of the chair seat.

The standard chair seat height is 475 mm for adults and 460 mm for children; this height plus the height from hips to the shoulder plus the length of arm, hand, and fingers will give us the height we need to consider for any position.

Residential Requirements

Application of these requirements does not apply, by force of the law, to private houses of any kind as mentioned before and are reviewed here to give you basic information that can be used to change an interior to make it more comfortable for elderly or wheelchair users as per their request.

All the measurements in building code come in millimeters. However, if you are still not comfortable with the metric system, you can use the conversion chart at the end of this chapter to change them to the imperial system.

Landscapes of the cities and residential areas are different, and based on their topography they can be almost flat or made on top of the cliffs with uphill and downhill roads which are almost unavoidable. People with limited movement ability will drive or will be driven to their residential building and then there are three ways to get into the home:

1. Elevator
2. Ramp
3. Passenger elevating device

In average houses, a ramp is the easiest way to make the entrance accessible, especially when the level of the ground floor is not more than 900 mm higher than the outside pathway.

When reached to the entrance hall, an elevator is the option to access to different levels if dealing with apartment buildings.

If the cost is not a problem, an elevator can be installed even in a multilevel house or town house which is very convenient for carrying furniture, suitcases, heavy everyday shopping, for the trip between different floors as well as a big help for the elderly or wheelchair users.

Ramp

- Should have a width of not less than 870 mm between hand rails, it can be increased to 1140 mm for a larger wheelchair specially when dealing with obese people.
- Should have a slope of not more than 1 in 12, or 1 in 20 because of the increased weight of the individual who is obese.
- Handle height should be 860 + 60 mm
- The maximum runoff a continuous ramp is 30 feet; beyond that length, ramps must have a flat rest area of at least 5 feet in length.

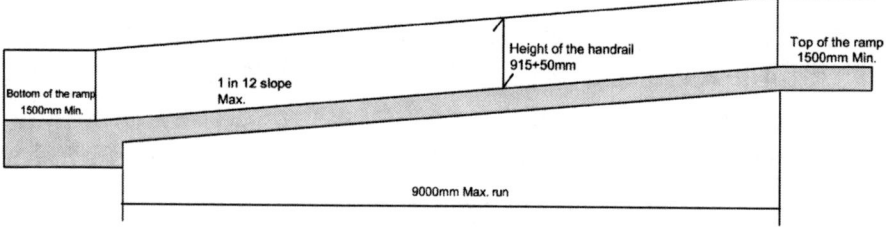

B-1

Corridors and any path of travel

- A 360-degree turn of a wheelchair requires a 150 cm = 5' – 0" diameter space.
- For instance, at the end of a dead-end corridor, enough space is needed for the turn back. See drawing B-2.
- A straight corridor should have a minimum of 110 cm = 3' – 8" width for easy wheelchair operation. To create enough space for a walking person to pass the wheelchair 5' – 0" wide corridor is needed.
  See drawing B-3
- A right angle turn needs a 110 cm = 3' – 8" radius for easy operation.
  See drawing B-4

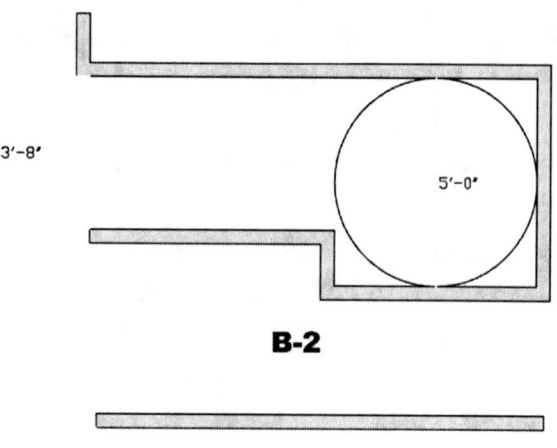

B-2

B-3

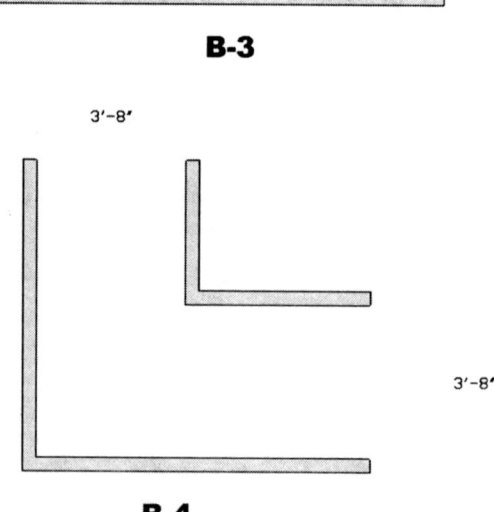

B-4

Keep in mind that any opening larger than 13 mm on the path can catch wheelchair wheels or canes, and it is necessary to find a solution to cover them or to reduce the size to max 13 mm.

Doorways:

- It is preferable that every doorway in a barrier-free path of travel shall have a clear opening width of a minimum of 850 mm when the door is fully opened, to allow a larger wheelchair or scooter get in and out of each room, but in any case, it shouldn't be less than 800 mm when the door is open.
- Door hardware should be installed between 900 mm and 1065 mm above the finished floor.
- No raised thresholds are preferred; however, where they are necessary or unavoidable, they must not exceed 13 mm in height above the finished floor surface.
- If the threshold is higher than 6 mm, it must be beveled to provide smooth transition from area to area.

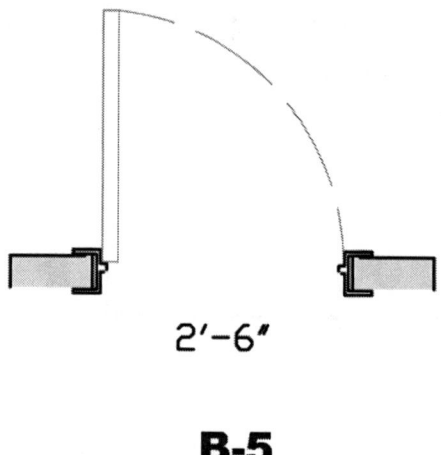

2'-6"

B-5

Washrooms

To make a washroom or bathroom accessible, make sure the following points are considered:

- Doorway clearance minimum 800 mm
- Turning diameter of 1500 mm or greater
- A transfer space of 900 to 1000 mm beside the toilet for those who use wheelchair
- Distance between the centerline of the toilet bowl and the side wall not less than 460 mm
- A rim height not more than 865 mm above the floor
- Mount toilet tissue dispenser sufficiently in front of the toilet to allow ease of access, and it should not interfere with grab bar use
- Consider a shallow sink with enough knee space beneath, not less than 760 mm wide and 735 mm height.
- Insulated pipes preferred otherwise there will be burn hazard.

- Soap dispenser and towel dispenser close to the lavatory (sink or basin), not more than 1200 mm above the floor and accessible to person in wheelchair
- Mirror mounted with its bottom edge not more than 1000 mm above the floor, or no more than 200 mm above the lavatory when measured from the surface of the sink or countertop
- Automatic water controls are the preferred alternative to levered handled faucets. However, single-lever faucet controls are preferred to separate hot and cold lever handles, both for basin and shower.

Shower

- Ensure that the dimensions of private showers are at least 1500 mm × 1500 mm (5'–0" × 5'–0").
- Texture: tiled open showers with floor drains are preferred; avoid enclosing walls, instead use shower curtains to allow for ease of access and assistance by caregivers, if needed.
- If using shower base, it must be beveled edge; in any case avoid curbs into accessible shower.
- Single-lever shower instead of a hot—and cold-lever faucet is preferred if automatic control faucet is not used. Temperature control and pressure control levers can be separate and is a preferred option.
- Use multiple, reinforced grab bars.
- An adjustable shower seat is a very convenient device for elderly people and useful for wheelchair users as they can move to the seat to take a shower.

Kitchen

The kitchen is a very important space in family and social life. In luxurious homes and kitchens, most probably there is enough room for wheelchair-bound people to move around the kitchen, but adjustable and pull-out work space, accessible shelves, and storage units with comfortable reach height and open under-counter with kneehole space will make the kitchen workable for wheelchair users and people with limited movement ability.

It is again a good idea to avoid sharp edges and slippery flooring.

A multilevel countertop with one comfortable level for wheelchair users with enough knee space is desirable. Many people eat while standing or sitting on stools beside the counter, and we can make it possible for all the family members, including the wheelchair-bound person to enjoy the family dinner at the same table.

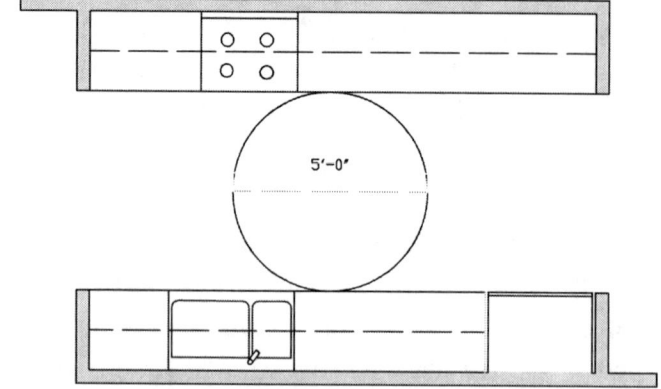

B-6

Living room, family room, and dining room

Space planning for these rooms will not be a big problem; just leave a 150 cm × 150 cm (5′ × 5′) empty space to enter any room and be sure that all the paths are not less than 3′ – 8″.

When space planning, include an empty space in the conversation area in the living and family room with enough space to handle the wheelchair.

In the dining room, remove one of the chairs and put the wheelchair instead, and make sure there is enough knee room under the table for the wheelchair user.

Bedroom

- Enough space to enter, exit, and maneuver comfortably is essential.
- On either sides or at least on one side of the bed at least 110 cm = 3′ – 8″ wide path is necessary.
- Grab bars may be useful on top of the bed to grasp and move back and forth or turn in the bed.

Metric conversion chart for the purpose of this book

When you know:	Multiply by:	To find:
Inches	25	millimeters
Feet	30	centimeters
Yards	0.9	Meters
Miles	1.6	kilometers
Centimeters	0.393	Inches
Meters	1.1	Yards
Kilometers	0.6	Miles

Chapter 4

Room by Room

Room by Room

In this part, we will walk through each functional area of an average home to review the importance of their function, and special points need to be considered in each area.

Plans with no furniture are provided for each room which will make you able to practice to arrange the furniture based on the client needs and wants. There are cutouts to use to practice on plans, or you can create your own cutouts also. You can use your ¼" = 1' – 0" furniture template to draw the outline of the furniture then you can add some details for a better presentation.

In these projects, some of the space-planning problems are easy to solve, while some are more complicated. Be patient and start with bubble diagrams to find a few options. Don't forget to check the traffic flow and then pick the one that you think is the best and try to arrange your furniture by sticking the cutouts to the paper or by the help of the furniture template.

To start, you can move around the cutouts to find the best place for that particular piece, mark the position, and then use the template to draw the lines.

There is no way to think that you should or should not have all the listed items in each room or to put them exactly with the minimum distance from each other. What is needed in a room is obviously up to you and your client.

To create something new, breaking the rules happens all the time. Some of the new ideas will end up in the garbage can as they don't offer any appealing new idea. They are just new without people and their needs in mind when designed. Once I was consulted by one of our friends who wanted to buy a new house in Vancouver. Everything about the building was fabulous, but the new layout of the main bathroom adjacent to the master bedroom surprised me! An open toilet bowl! The bathroom was open to the bedroom, and a pony wall with two wide openings on both sides of the short wall was the only divider between the bathroom and bedroom. On the other hand, there was no door or divider between the toilet bowl and bathroom; as a result, the toilet bowl was part of the bedroom! The layout arrangement was difficult and expensive to change and was the only reason why the house was not being able to be sold.

Some of the new ideas will change the design world as it happened in the past and will happen in the future—new ideas like open plans which were introduced in early twentieth century and are still is in use in the twenty-first century.

Be creative, but try to learn and practice the basics. Later you will be able to proceed with new ideas.

Everything named or discussed here is a guide to start in the design field. Keep in mind that all the dimensions noted here are based on the human scale, thus you can add to them when you have enough room, but you cannot reduce them. For example, if you design a 50 cm (20") wide hallway, nobody will be able to pass comfortably and it will not be approved by any building code or responsible authority.

Each room, as regards to its function, needs proper furniture which is arranged to meet the main function of the room and to create a relaxing, comfortable space to live and work in.

In this part of the book, under the name of each room, you will gain some information about:

- the furniture usually needed in a room
- special points to consider
- space requirements
- barrier-free consideration
- sample plan to work with
- cutouts of furniture
- You are expected to start to space plan the rooms. At the end, when you are finished with the rooms, you will have the opportunity to put everything you learned together to create and draw a new space planning design for the final project. When you are done with your design, you will be able to compare

yours with one of the good solutions for that particular space. Considering the principle of design and the list of needs and wants, you can judge which one is better and why. Analyze and critic both of the designs, yours and the given sample, it is the best way to enrich your space planning experience.

Foyer

The entrance space is where you are welcomed when entering the house. It is also where overcoats, raincoats, and umbrellas are hanged, shoes and boots are removed, and that is why it should be both beautiful and functional.

- Closet or hanger for clothes
- Closet or hanger for footwear
- Drawer or credenza for purses, gloves, scarves
- Chair, bench, settee
- Console table
- Mirror
- Rug or mat to rub the shoes to get rid of dust, dirt, and mud
- Decorative rug
- Artworks like paintings, statues
- Floor accessories like standing lamps, vases . . .
- Plants (if there is not enough natural light, you can use artificial plants and flowers)

These are different things you can choose to have in a foyer, and depending on how big the space is, some of them must be there and some are optional.

Pick easy-to-clean flooring material as this is the first area to be wet or dirty, especially on a rainy day.

Always search for eco-friendly materials to use as they are good for health as well as the earth.

If you are designing for people with limited movement ability, you should consider barrier-free design options. Your local building code is the best to check. The "Barrier-Free Design" section of this book may help you for generality. The main rule is that the dimensions should be easy to use for people on wheelchair.

No door's width should be less than 800 mm, and no hallway's width less than 920 mm.

Powder Room

A powder room is considered as both private and public space, as in some houses it is used mostly by guests, and in some, it is an everyday use space by the residents.

The powder room is not just a place to wash, but it can be a beautiful, fully decorated place to use while it is serving the main function.

The smallest space needed for a powder room is 3' – 0" × 6' – 6" or 4' – 6" × 4' – 6" which will change to 5' – 0" × 5' – 0" for wheelchair users, while a luxury powder room can be as big as an average room in a house.

The following utilities are mandatory in a regular powder room:

- Lavatory sink (basin)
- Toilet bowl
- Towel holder
- Toilet tissue holder
- Mirror
- Lighting fixtures (functional or decorative)

The following can be added to what you already have in this space:

- Small trash holder
- Plants and flowers (natural or artificial)
- Artwork
- Handmade decorative items
- Candles

Women carry their purses to the powder room to freshen up, so it is a good idea to have hooks or racks if the vanity top doesn't have enough room or doesn't exist, which will happen when you have a pedestal sink.

It is better to have lighting fixtures on either side of the mirror as well as along the top to create a shadow-free reflection in the mirror.

Water-saving toilets with dual flush are a green choice.

LED and the other energy-saving bulbs are environmentally friendly choices for lighting.

A minimum of sixteen-inch space is needed between the centerline of the toilet bowl to the wall.

If designing for people on wheelchair, you have to have enough room to maneuver and the other requirements discussed in the barrier-free design section.

Home Office

The need of having a computer or a laptop at home is increased; people use the Internet to keep in touch with friends and family around the globe. Online banking, online reservation, and online shopping are getting more popular. If one wants to keep abreast of the news and in sync with the fast-changing times, it really becomes hard to avoid having a computer at home.

The vast use of computers has made it possible for people to work at home or from home in different criteria. Whether wrong or right, people manage to work after-hours through their laptops or cell phones at home.

All these new ideas have resulted in a strong need for having a home office as a separate room or as a part of another room.

To be able to "space plan" a home office:

- Determine the main user of this area.
- Determine who else will be sharing the space.
- Make a list of every equipment and furniture which is needed in this office.
- Determine how much space is needed to keep or store papers, samples, or any other job-related materials.

- Look for enough lighting and power outlets as they needed to hook up different equipments and to work comfortably. Computer, printer, fax machine, paper shredder, telephone set, and table lamps are among the equipments which should be connected to the electrical outlet or data outlet (Internet cable).

Furniture needed in an office usually is a desk, including a computer desk and drafting desk, chairs, built-in or freestanding storage units like shelves, cabinets, and armoire.

Ergonomic chairs with the correct height are the best to use in the office which are a big help to have a good posture and a healthier body with no pain.

The overall look of the office and selected furniture should flow with the home, and remember to keep this look professional.

The space between desk and wall units should be 42" – 48".

To pull out the drawers of a file cabinet, a 30" – 36" space in front of the cabinet is needed.

It is wonderful if you have the luxury of an entire room devoted to a home office but if not, a drop-lid desk part of a room storage wall unit can be a small home office by pulling up a chair from everywhere and when finished, the writing surface flips up and will blend into the wall unit. This unit can be in any room as well as the kitchen.

Kitchen

Some people say "kitchen is the heart of the home." Whether one agrees or not, the kitchen is a very important part of people's everyday life as well as their social life.

A well-organized kitchen saves a lot of time and energy when in use for cooking and serving.

In twentieth—and twenty-first-century, the idea of open plans developed and turned to be a popular trend used everywhere. kitchens were designed to be a part of family room or a part of living room.

Although the kitchen's main function is a place meant for cooking, even medium-sized kitchens often serve other functions. A small eating area (nook) adjacent to the kitchen is for serving breakfast and casual dining; homework and small school projects can happen in this space too. If there is enough room, it is possible to create a small office inside the kitchen for the goddess of the home. In this case, a surface to fit the laptop and a couple of drawers to keep the paperwork are enough.

> A triangle shaped by three lines between the stove and refrigerator, the refrigerator and sink, and the sink and stove is called the "working triangle," and it is a tool to check if the kitchen is comfortable to work in. The perimeter of this triangle should not exceed 20' – 0".

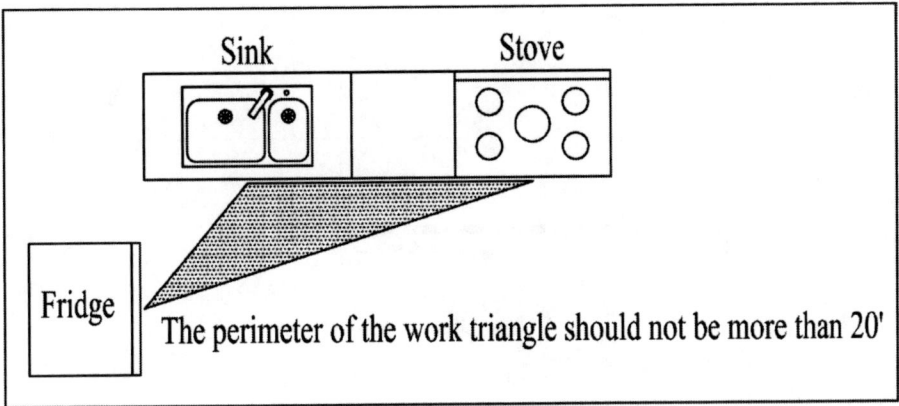

The kitchen arrangement can be U shape, Center isle (parallel), L shape, or L shape with a center island. It all depends on the size and the shape of the space.

Check the market for a vast variety of products to pick what you or your clients think is the best to serve the purpose.

- Cabinets (Metal, Wood, HDF)
- Sink or sinks (single, double or one and a half)
- Fridge
- Freezer
- Combination of fridge and freezer on top of each other or side by side
- Range, electric or gas cooktop, stove
- Microwave
- Speed oven (combination of microwave function for defrosting and heating and cooking oven with conventional mode and browning elements)
- Wall oven
- Dishwasher
- Ventilation hood
- Wine cooler

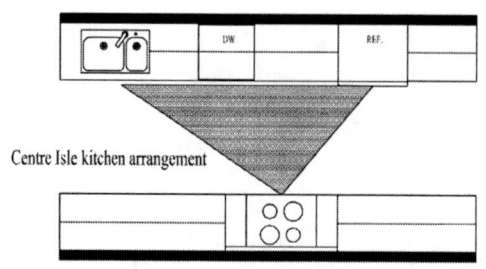

Centre Isle kitchen arrangement

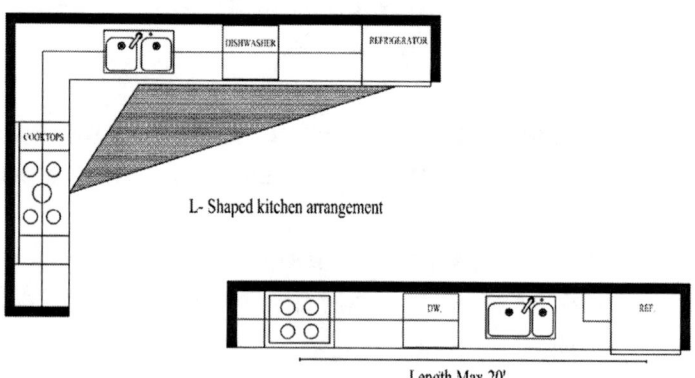

L- Shaped kitchen arrangement

Length Max.20'

Single Line kitchen arrangement

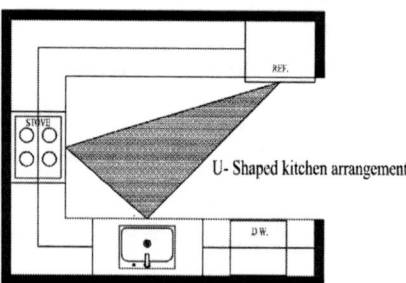

U- Shaped kitchen arrangement

These are equipments that you can arrange to have in a modern kitchen.

Most of the kitchen companies and cabinet makers offer design service which can be very helpful. It is necessary to pick your appliances before putting the drawings to final form as the size of the appliances will dramatically change your design.

If the fridge has an ice maker, watch for the convenient way to hook it up to the water supply.

Avoid putting the microwave above the stove.

General lighting—under the cabinet and over the island lighting—are needed for comfortable preparing, cooking, serving, and eating in the kitchen.

If there is any need for a barrier-free design, consultation with professionals is required. If misused or improperly used, hot water, cooktop flame, heat, gas, and electricity make the kitchen a very dangerous place.

Thinking green when designing a kitchen will create a healthier environment and will save money for the family as well.

In the chapter "Accessible and Green," you can find more information about an eco-friendly kitchen.

Great Room/Family Room

The term "great room" is used to describe the function of a large, open-concept space that serves more than one function. In many modern homes, the great room is the most popular gathering place in the house where the family spends time in the evening and on weekends.

When there is no need or there is not enough space to have a separate formal living room, family room and eating area, designer combines all these functions into a single living space called great room which is also open to the kitchen. It may or may not have an adjacent formal dining room.

Great room décor is casual and inviting. A fireplace is a popular focal point for this multifunctional room of the house.

Following are the facilities used to divide different functions from each other or to define each function in this open-space room:

- Furniture, including sofa, love seat, chair, sofa table, coffee table, side table, computer desk.
- Architectural elements like fireplace, pony wall, glass, metal and wood dividers, island and bottom cabinet.
- Accessories as area rug, plant, statue, standing lamps.

It is the responsibility of a space planner to find out who the real users of this space are, what is happening in each area, and what items and which moods are necessary to fulfill the client's needs and wants.

Never overwhelm the room, as in real life people will bring more items to these areas as time goes on. Toys, books, magazines, souvenirs, plants, and flowers are just a few among them.

If size and shape of the plan allows you, create a separate spot for watching TV from the conversation area.

When space planning a great room, pay more attention to the proportion of the pieces and the balance you want to create. A three-dimensional consideration is necessary as you want to see the whole room united and in harmony.

Try to avoid huge pieces which can block part of the room and will make it small, visually unbalanced, and uncomfortable.

Do not put a huge sofa very close to the dining area with table and chairs as it creates a visually heavy spot and is hard to be balanced with smaller pieces.

Formal Living Room

A formal living room is a place to entertain people in a more formal manner. It usually happens when family members don't want to share the privacy of kitchen and family room with the guests or when they need more room to get together with family and friends to enjoy the night in special occasions like Christmas or a thanksgiving dinner.

In most of the recently built houses, a formal living room is smaller than the family room as it is used less often. The furniture can be modern or traditional but usually is finer and more delicate than what is used in the family room.

Depending on the desired mood and style you want to convey, you could chose between elegant modern furniture and classic furniture. If you plan to have a mix style that can be visually pleasing, keep it moderate. Extremely mixed furniture styles appear jarring and inharmonious.

More expensive pieces of decorative items and antiques can find a showcase in this room.

Hardwood, stone tile, high quality ceramic tiles are all good flooring materials for this room. A fine silk rug on the floor and quality artworks hanged on the wall will bring the sense of formality to this space.

A fireplace, a big piece of artwork, or a gorgeous outside view, these are all suitable to be the focal point of this space. Furniture arrangement should also impart a sense of formality.

Mellow ambient light plus task light of table lamps and accent light shining on artworks can create a dramatic mood in this room.

Dining Room

A *dining room* serves different purposes for different people. For some, it is used to hold formal functions or get-togethers during the holidays and some other special occasions like birthdays and anniversaries. For some, it is an everyday dining area for the family, while for some others, on top of the other functions, it is a place to work.

A dining table is the focal point of the dining room.

Dining tables are available in different shapes and styles. Rectangular, square, round, oval, and octagon tables are available in variety of sizes for serving from two up to sixteen people.

The length of the dining tables may vary as well as their width, but most of the rectangular tables have a width of 28"-42".

Round tables mostly come in:

- 36"- 44" diameter for four persons
- 44"-54" diameter for four to six persons
- 60"-70" diameter for six to eight persons

In general, each person requires about 24 inches (60 cm) in width, and you should leave about 4-6 inches (10-15 cm) in between.

Keep the table at least 24 inches (60cm) away from the wall on all sides.

Chairs are different in size, shape, and style but to seat around the table a minimum of 36-inch space needed for people to pull out the chair, get in, sit comfortably, and eat. It is necessary to increase this minimum distance if the chairs are very big or if there is something on the wall that should be protected from the chairs' kick.

In the dining room, you may design to have a buffet to display china, crystal, and silverware; it can come without display windows just to serve as a cabinet to keep the tableware. If there is any drawer, leave enough room in front of the drawers to make it possible to pull them out comfortably.

A small table can be used for serving drinks.

The best place to hang a crystal chandelier is above and in the middle of the dining table if creating a more traditional or a classic look is the target.

Chandeliers with modern design are available in the market and can be used in a contemporary style interior.

A centerpiece for the table is always attractive. A beautiful flower arrangement, natural or artificial, candles sitting on sand or pebbles, or a crystal bowl of water with floating candles, flowers, or green leaves are all beautiful. Any creative idea is welcome as long as it is in proportion with the table, lighting fixture, and the other items used in this space. For instance, if you plan to keep the centerpiece on the table while serving dinner, the centerpiece shouldn't be very tall, thereby obstructing people's ability to look at and talk to each other. Also, if the chandelier is hanging down, a tall flower arrangement is not appropriate.

Mirrors will make the room more spacious and luxurious. In a classic setting, a tall mirror in a decorative frame can stand against the wall at the end of the dining table's length, and smaller mirrors can be hanged on the wall or on mantle top of the fireplace. If there is any spectacular view, it is a smart idea to hang a mirror to reflect the view, thus making it visible from more angles. Artworks and antiques are proper to use as decorative items in a dining room.

People on wheelchair can easily share the same dining table by removing one or two chairs just if there is enough knee room under the table.

Do not forget to check the traffic path to be sure of its accessibility for the wheelchair users.

Bathroom

An old utilitarian space called bathroom changed to a private sanctuary where people can wash, relax, read, listen to the music, and enjoy their time in a complete privacy. In the same time for some busy couples to be able to share the bathroom in the morning is a very important factor as they want to get ready to go to work. In some houses, kids share the bathroom with parents. These conflicting interests should be solved before any serious decision about bathroom layout, finishing, and fixtures.

Before starting any bathroom project, make your questionnaire ready and ask these questions:

- How many people will use this space?
- How many storage rooms do you need?
- Is there any kid sharing the bathroom with parents?
- Is there any elderly person to use this space?
- How often will a bathtub be used?
- Is just a large, comfortable modern shower booth enough?
- If the space is not enough for both, which one do you prefer to have? A double lavatory sink or a whirlpool?
- Do you need or like to have a luxury shower with steam shower, body spray, and rain showerhead?
- Do you have any style, design preference, or particular color scheme in your mind?

To start planning for a bathroom, consider the minimum space requirements to make the space comfortable to use.

- Space in front of a toilet Min: 24"
- Space between a toilet bowl and side wall Min: 10"
- Space in front of a bathtub Min: 36"
- Space for shower booth Min: 36" × 36"

There are 32" × 32" shower bases available in the market; use them just if the bathroom is too small and if a compact design is necessary. Remember that most of the people use this space every day, at least once, while the bathtub or whirlpool is a luxury addition which is ideal to have but will be used occasionally and in some cases once a year or never. The homeowner's answers in your questionnaire will tell you what the priorities are.

- Deck space around sink approximately 30"
- Deck space between two sinks approximately 25"

Sink, faucet, toilet, tub, showerhead, and lighting fixture, vanity and vanity top are the major fixtures in a bathroom. Flooring material, wall covering for general area and wet area like shower booth and tub surrounding, door and window, hardware and shower curtain also are important items to select for a bathroom.

All the finishing material and fixtures should work together to impart functionality and beauty to this important room of the house.

To visit showrooms or review some home and design magazines are necessary activities to keep oneself updated and knowledgeable about new products and trends.

Tub

When picking a bathtub, the following options are available in the market:

- Alcove tub (to be installed between three walls)
- Freestanding or footed tub
- Platform tub (flash with a platform built in the bathroom)
- In-ground tub (flash with the bathroom floor)
- Deep soaking tub
- Air-jetted tub (whirlpool)

Sink

You have some choices for the proper sink in your bathroom when ready to select one.

- Pedestal sinks that stand on a basic or highly decorative column
- Wall-mounted sinks (the best choice for barrier-free bathrooms)
- Console sinks which are wall-mounted with two extra legs in front
- Under-mount sinks which sit below the surface of the vanity countertop. Under-mount sinks maximize the amount of clear vanity top space which will come handy for keeping everyday use items.

- Self-rimmed sinks which will have their rims overlapping the countertop surface, while the basin (washing bowl) sits below the vanity countertop.
- Integral sink (vanity countertop and the sink are molded seamlessly.)
- Vessel sinks which resemble a bowl sits on the vanity top and are becoming one of the most popular designed sink options. Some people are not happy with the fact that water, dirt, and soap scum should be cleaned from both inside and outside of the basin while they can rinse inside but not the outside.

Faucet

There are hundreds of options from basic to deluxe modern models when it is time to shop for faucets and faucet spouts.

Faucets come in different finishes. Common finishes are chrome, polished chrome, satin brass, and brass. Luxury finishes can be gold or platinum.

Motion-sensor faucets which are very hygienic are a new trend. They appeared in commercial buildings many years ago, but new versions are less expensive and designed for residential projects. It can come with the kitchen sink as well as the lavatory basin in the bathroom or the powder room.

This kind of faucet is very user-friendly and a magnificent feature, especially if there is any user with limited ability to work with his or her hand including a child, a disabled person, or an elderly person with arthritis or pain.

Toilet bowl and tank

Toilet can come in one piece or two pieces (bowl and tank) and usually the first option is more expensive than the other one.

Dual-flush toilets are considered green design as they come with an option of being able to use less water if the full capacity is not needed.

Style, color, height, and size variety in the market make you able to pick the best available toilet for your design.

Flooring

Ceramic, stone, concrete, wood, and carpet all have a good reputation as floor coverings in the bathroom. The most important point is as to who is using the space and how often they use it. What is the level of care and cleaning in that particular household?

A carpet is not recommended due to high maintenance characteristic and can be used if there is no water splashing or water leaking.

Wood, especially bamboo, which is more water resistant can work as a flooring material, but it is not as safe and comfortable to use as ceramic and stone. If you prefer the appearance of the wood but not the nature of the wood, there are some ceramic tiles which their pattern, texture, and color resembling that of wood.

When the shower base is custom-made and built-in, floor tiles should be non-slip with small dimension to make it easy to provide 1.5%-3% floor slope to drain the water from the shower base.

Mosaic and stone tiles are available in small square shapes 1" × 1", 2" × 2", and 3" × 3" or small rectangular shape of usually 1" × 2" or 3".

Glass tiles are not the best for the floor, but their aquatic effect is very pleasant on the walls. They come in different sizes, colors, and shapes like square, rectangle, and circle.

Pebbled mosaic tiles are available in the market and come in a 12" × 12" sheet. Pebbles are sitting side by side, stuck on a flexible plastic mesh to form a ready-to-install tile.

The shower booth's curb can be covered by bathroom floor tile or smaller shower base tile.

Wall covering

Ceramic and stone tiles, also glass mosaics, are the best wall covering material in bathrooms as they are water resistant and are available in different sizes, colors, and texture to satisfy any design preferences.

Washable wall paper and wood are suitable for any wall in the bathroom except in the shower booth and tub surrounding.

Semi-glass paint is the less expensive option and the proper way to cover walls in a bathroom, but still ceramic and stone tile or mosaics are needed to cover the wet surfaces.

Vanity and mirror

Every sink if it is not pedestal, consol, or wall mount needs a vanity to sit in or sit on. Vanity can provide storage room to keep the bath room inventory as well as daily use items.

When designing a vanity, it is possible to include a cabinet, shelf, and drawer.

Mirror is a must to install above the vanity and can be functional or decorative, with or without a frame. A general rule is not to exceed the length of the vanity.

Beveled edge mirrors with the same length as vanity are modern and stylish but not cheap.

Vanity top

When selecting a vanity top for the bathroom which is the wettest room in the house, the two most important considerations are: water-resistance of the material and its ease of cleaning.

Solid surfaces, including natural stones like granite and marble or man-made stones, like quartz stone and Corian, are all commonly used and should be sealed and treated to prevent water damage and stains.

Laundry Room

Laundry space can be as small as a closet just to put the washer and dryer on top of each other. In this case, watch for the door to swing outward or use a folding door which doesn't take too much room when open.

Design a laundry closet at least 15" wider than the size of the machines, and you will have enough space to install shelves to keep the detergent, drier sheets, or everything else which is useful to have beside the washer and drier.

In larger houses, the laundry room can be big enough to provide room for a deep sink to hand-wash some items if necessary, an ironing table, and even a sewing machine. In this case table or counter to fold the cloths, hanging rod and more storage units can be added to the room as needed.

Limit the decorative items to framed artworks and plants (natural or artificial). Keep everything simple and easy to clean.

Non-slippery ceramic tile is the best material for flooring.

Ambient light and task lights are needed to make it possible to work comfortably.

Look for the Energy Star label when you pick the washer and drier to save some energy.

Efficient ventilation for drier is needed. Consultation with professionals is necessary for both plumbing and ventilation system.

Reach height, traffic pattern, and maneuver space are subject to close attention if there is any wheelchair user at home.

Children's Room

To space plan a room for a child or children in a family house, the number of kids in a room and their age are the most influential information you need for your design. A preliminary "planned" layout of the room is essential before installing any storage or purchasing the bed, drawer, or other pieces of furniture and equipments.

Direct sunlight and fresh air is essential for any bedroom, especially for kids' room.

If being designed for a baby, the size of the bed is small, but you need a surface for changing the diaper with a shelf close by for necessary items like cleaning tissues, baby powder, Vaseline, and to keep the nappies or diapers.

An infant's (less than one-year-old) bed should be fully enclosed by high side rails to protect the baby. Designing a room for *toddlers* (one—to three-year-olds) calls for a big toy box or enough deep drawers to keep the room tidy and the toys clean. A toddler bed is a small bed designed for the safety of toddlers and is used as a transitional bed between an infant and an ordinary twin bed. Commonly, these beds have low side rails on both sides, possibly removable, to prevent the child from accidentally rolling out of the bed while sleeping. The size of the mattress is often the same size as that in baby bed.

A junior bed size is 149 × 72 cm and usually has a short side rail on top part of the bed along the side

A desk for doing homework and a small table for finishing school projects seems necessary in this room if there is enough space.

Books, stationeries, toys, clothes, collections of favorite items need a preplanned shelving system for a perfect look and a well-organized room.

In kids' room, an easy-to-wash flooring material like any kind of hard surface plus a removable carpet or rug is better than a wall-to-wall carpet that can keep dirt and dust and is not easy to remove and wash.

Teenagers needed more storage space, a computer desk, and a twin or double bed. Extra long mattresses and beds are available for tall teenagers.

For an accurate space planning the important dimensions are the mattress size depends on the style and shape of the bed.

The actual bed size will be different and should be considered when planning a bedroom.

Mattress size

Twin/single: 39" × 75"

Extra long twin/single: 39" × 80"

Double (full): 54" × 75"

Extra long double: 54" × 80"

This group (teenagers) will spend more time in their room than the other age groups as they start to be independent and don't need to be with their parents most of the time.

When designing for more than two kids in a room, it is possible to have two twin beds, a bunk bed, or a trundle bed.

There are a variety of beds available in the market to choose from to fulfill the needs and dreams of your clients.

- A bunk bed is two or more beds, one atop the other.
- An infant's bed (also crib or cot) is a small bed specifically for babies and infants.
- A daybed is a couch that is used as a seat by day and as a bed by night.
- A futon is a traditional style of Japanese bed that is also available in a larger Western style.
- A Murphy bed is a bed that can hinge into a wall or cabinet to save space.

- A platform bed is a mattress resting on a solid, flat raised surface, either freestanding or part of the structure of the room.
- A sofa bed is a bed that is stored inside a sofa and acts as both.
- A trundle bed or truckle bed is a bed usually stored beneath a twin bed.

Master Bedroom

A master bedroom is normally designed for a couple. It can be a sanctuary for a good night sleep or a multitask space to do the office work, to read, to exercise as well as change and get ready to go, watch TV, and sleep. During the design process, the most important point is to identify these needs and to space plan accordingly.

You can select furniture pieces in any size, color, and style. Just try to coordinate different pieces to create a sense of balance and unity.

Make sure all pieces are necessary and will not make the room crowded and packed with furniture.

You may or may not have window treatment in the other rooms, but most probably, for the privacy and light control reason, it is needed in the master bedroom.

The focal point of the master bedroom is the bed and will remain the same, no matter how many more functions are running in this space.

Beds are available in a vast variety of sizes and styles; it can be just a mattress on a same size spring box and frame. The bed can have a headboard, footboard, two or four posts or even a wide platform. Mattress sizes however do not have this much variety and are standard.

Mattress dimensions in inches

Size	USA and Canada	Europe
Twin/single	39W × 75L	36W × 75L
Double/full	54W × 75L	54W × 75L
Queen	60W × 80L	72 W × 75L
King	76W × 80L	60 W × 75L
California king	72W × 84L	—

Extra large sizes in twin and full are available that are five inches longer than the regular one.

Twin/single XL is 39" × 80".

Double/full XL is 54" × 80".

Olympic/expanded queen is wider and longer than queen 66"W × 80"L.

Super king is a European size and the dimensions are 72"W × 78"L.

Grand king is popular in USA and Canada which is 80"W × 98"L.

Pillows

Standard pillow size is 20″ × 26″ and is the most common size pillow which is fit for twin, double, and queen-size mattresses.

King-size pillow is 20″ × 36″, suitable for king and California king.

Euro size pillow is 26″ × 26″.

The master bedroom is usually bigger than the other bedrooms and needs more storage space. Deep, long closets with inside dividers and drawers should provide enough room to hang the long and short dresses. In order to have an organized room, folded sweaters, pants and shirts, purses, shoes, hats, socks, and the other belongings all need their own special place.

Master Bedroom Suite

A master bedroom often has an adjacent private bathroom, and in this case it will be called the master bedroom suite.

Designing an open bathroom adjacent to the master bedroom is getting popular because of the different look. The new very decorative and well-designed tub, faucets, vessel sinks, lighting fixtures, and bathroom accessories encourage the open plan. The most used item to define these two spaces from each other is a two—or three-sided fireplace which can be beautiful and functional both. However a high level of maintenance and cleaning is needed to keep this space neat and clean.

A toilet should be enclosed regardless of the design.

The other popular trend is to have a walk-in closet in a master bedroom suite. Well-designed walk-in closets are important aspects of any master suite. A walk-in closet is often set with an easy access to bedroom.

A truly good walk-in closet design should integrate the closet space harmoniously with the owner's needs and wants and can be custom-made.

If there is enough space to enjoy a luxury design, it is possible to have two different walk-in closets, one for her and one for him. It is a smart idea to force fresh air into the walk-in closet or to provide a window for this room and if not possible install an exhaust fan in order to have fresh air with no smell all the time.

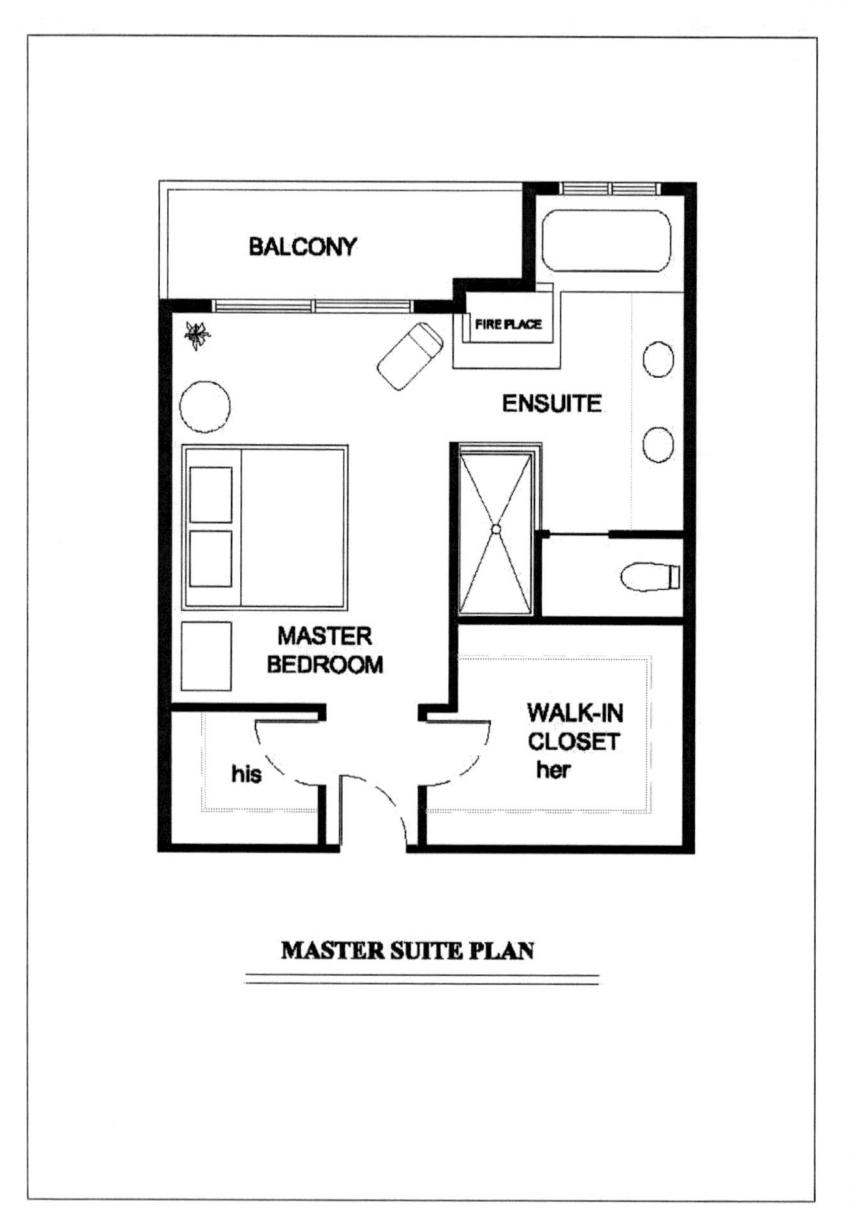

Put Everything Together

You learned about elements and principles of design and the design process for residential interior space planning. Besides, you had the opportunity to review the requirements for each functional area in an average home.

You know how to collect the client's needs and wants.

You already practiced to measure, sketch, bubble diagram, and pick your favorite design.

You are familiar with drawing tools and know how to scale and how to draw.

Assignment Plans

Now it is time to put everything together and to start to space plan for these actual rooms of a house.

Some scaled furniture and appliances' cutouts are provided to use for your design.

Don't forget that they are some of the standard size pieces, but you are free to use any kind of furniture, appliances, and bathroom fixtures.

You can use your 1/4" = 1' – 0" furniture template; you can have the measurement of your favorite pieces to draw them in the plan or to make your own template as well as working with pre-made cutout which is available at the end of this chapter.

The client:

Your client is a family of four people.

Fred, the father, works out of home but needs an office space at home.

Liz, the mother, is an interior designer. She works from home and needs a home office with proper storage for samples and client files and a table to work on.

Fred and Liz can share the home office but need two different workstations. They also have to have a copy/fax/phone machine.

Fred and Liz have walk-in closets and an en suite bath adjacent to their master bedroom which doesn't need any change, and they love it the way it is. They have a king-size bed which they want to keep it.

They love to entertain family and friends.

The formal dining room is adjacent to the great room and needs to hold at least ten seating around the table.

Their daughters, nine-year-old Sara and four-year-old Hanna, will share the kids' room.

The bathroom plan should be space planned for two kids. The client prefers to have a double sink.

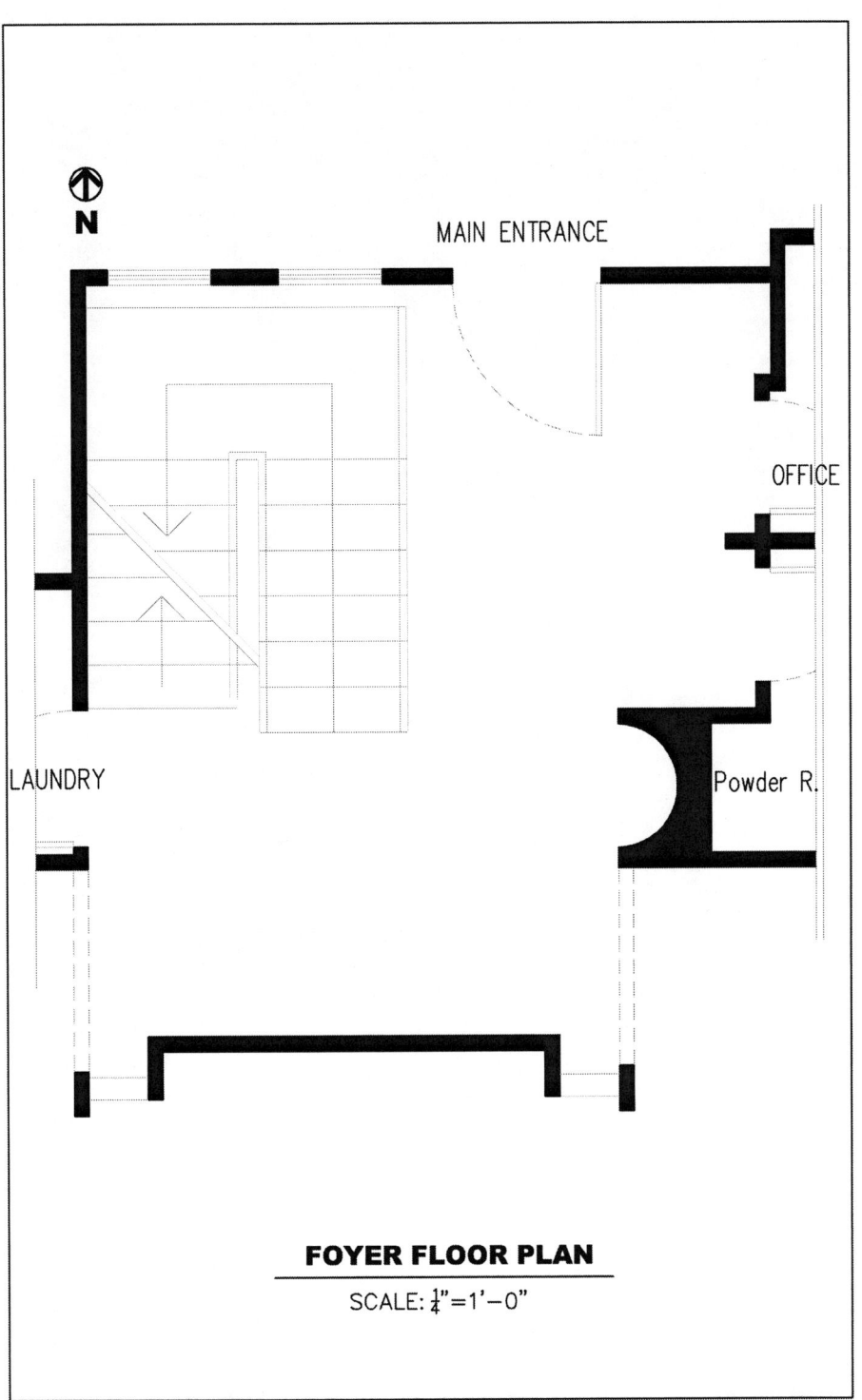

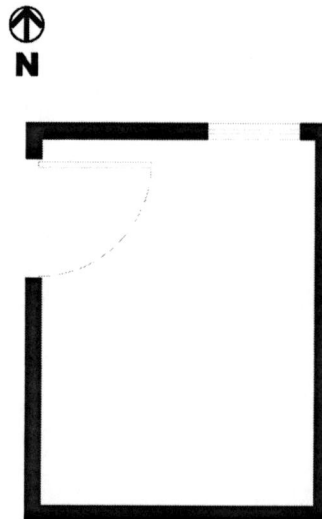

POWDER ROOM PLAN

SCALE: $\frac{1}{4}"=1'-0"$

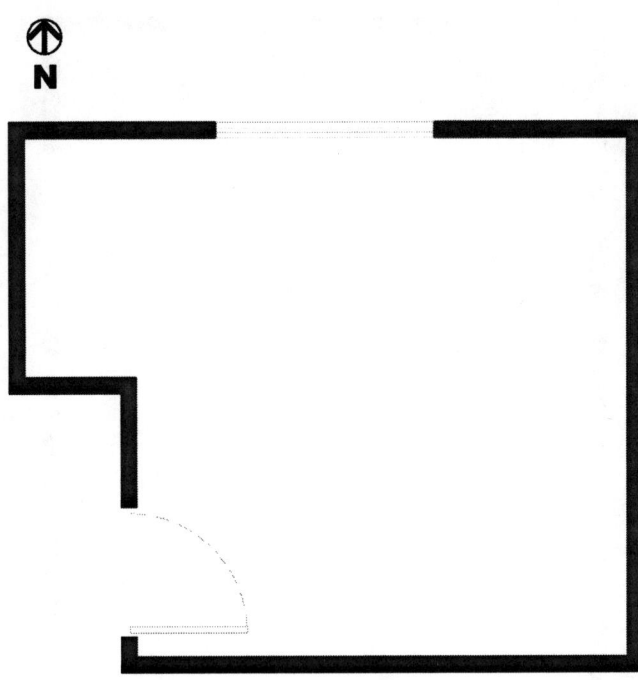

HOME OFFICE PLAN

SCALE : $\frac{1}{4}"=1'-0"$

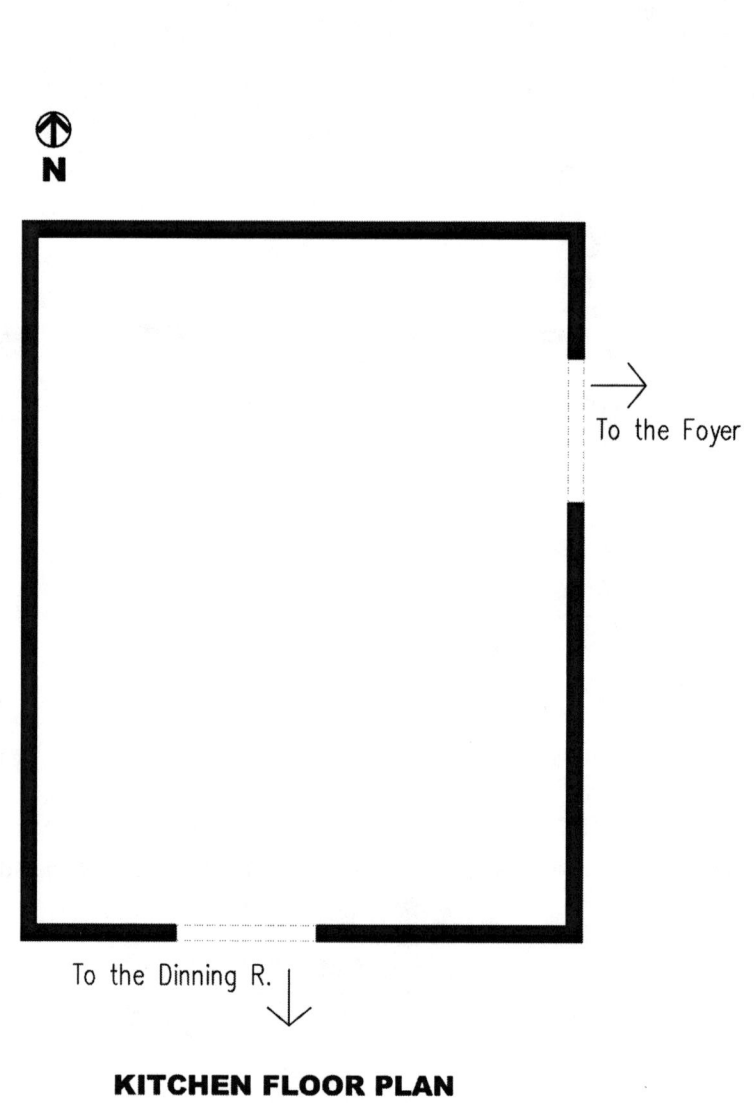

KITCHEN FLOOR PLAN

SCALE: $\frac{1}{4}"=1'-0"$

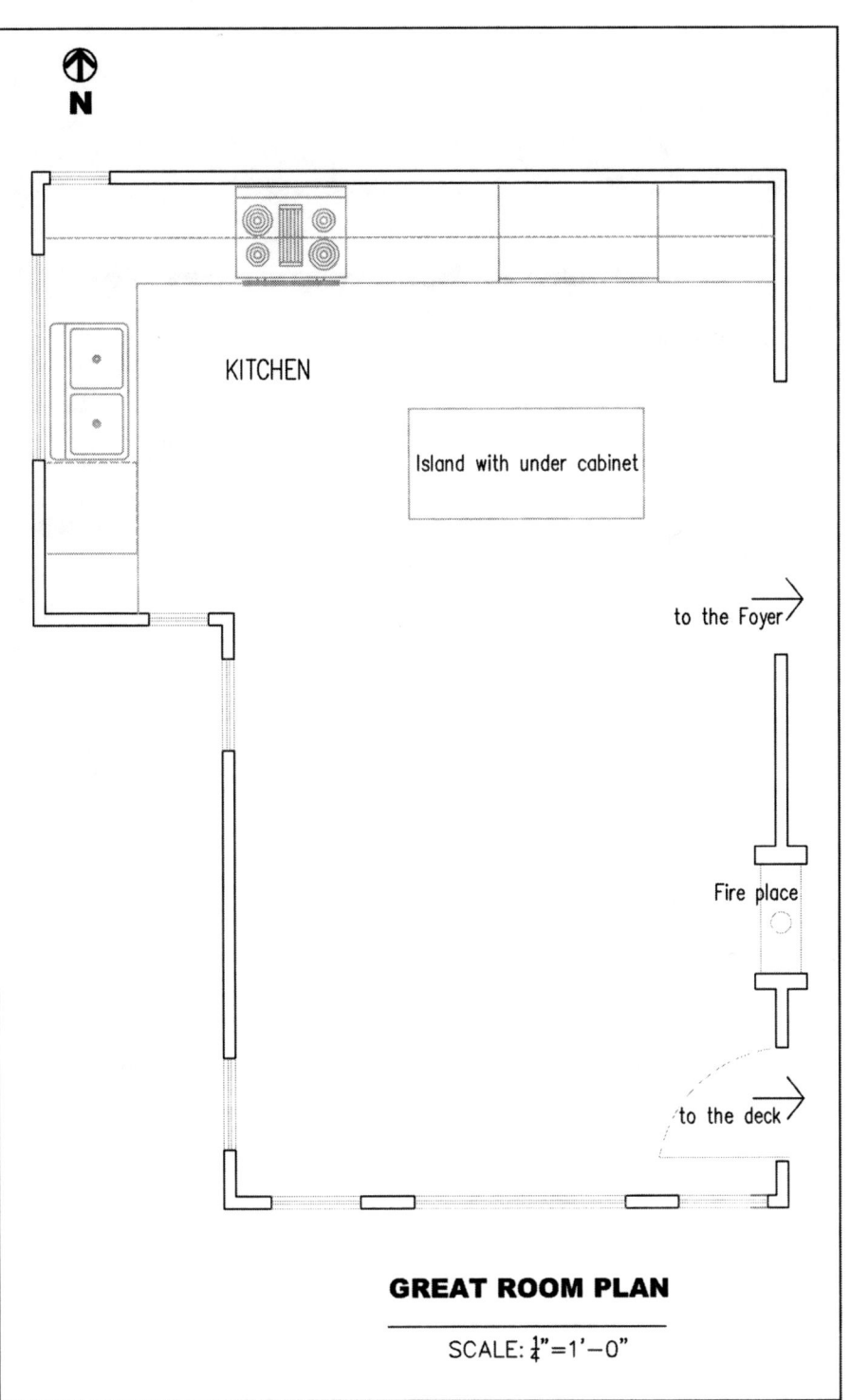

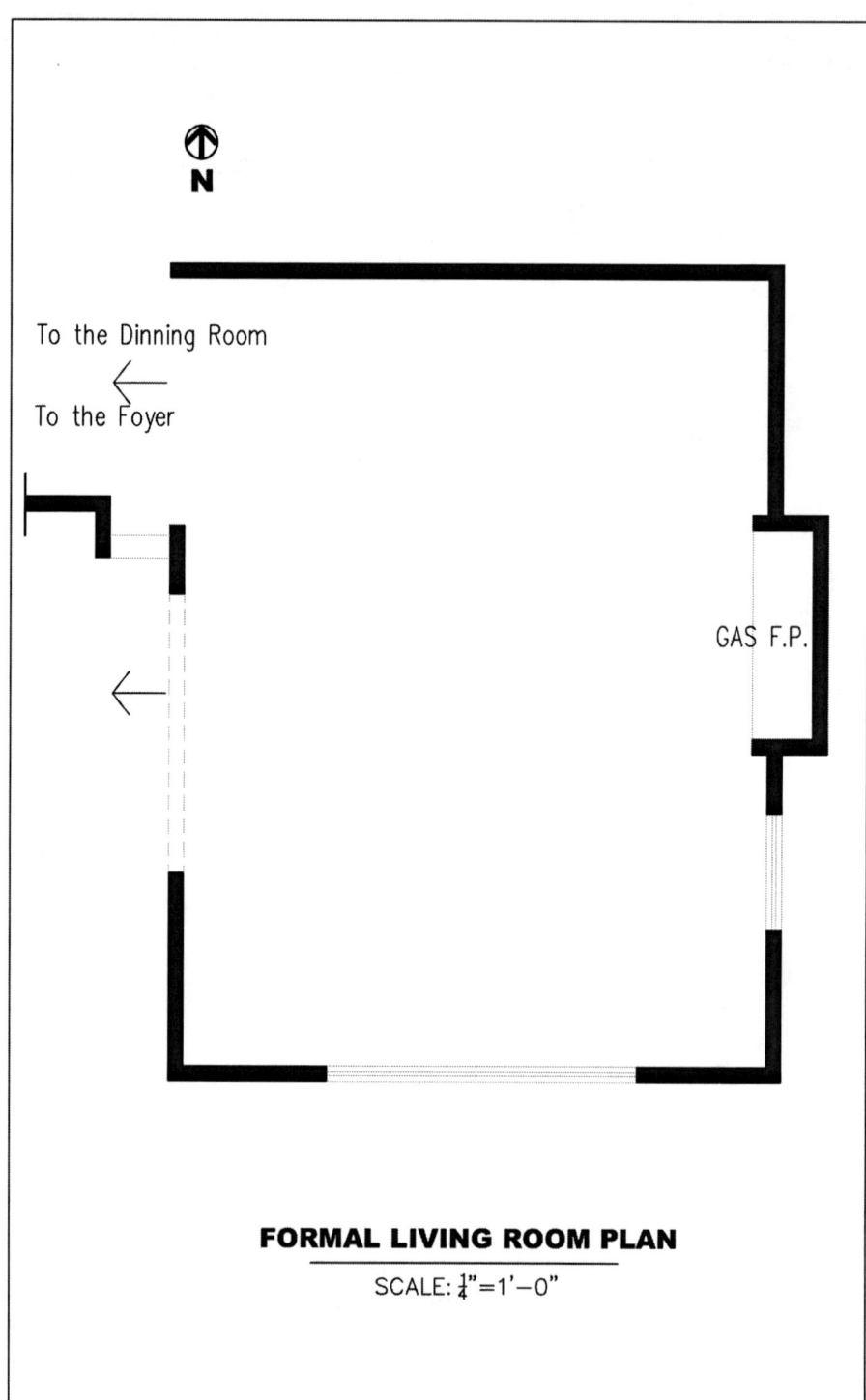

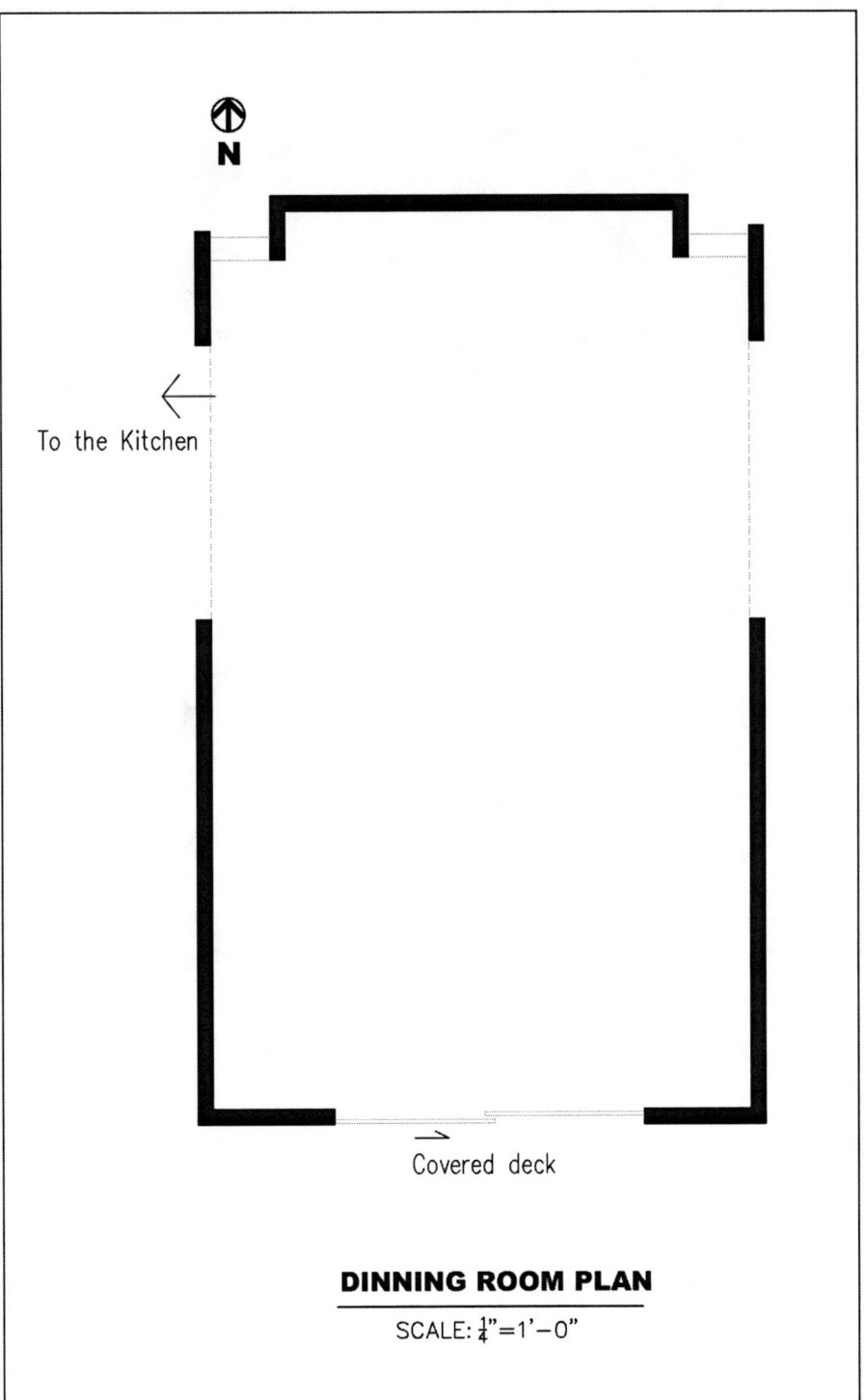

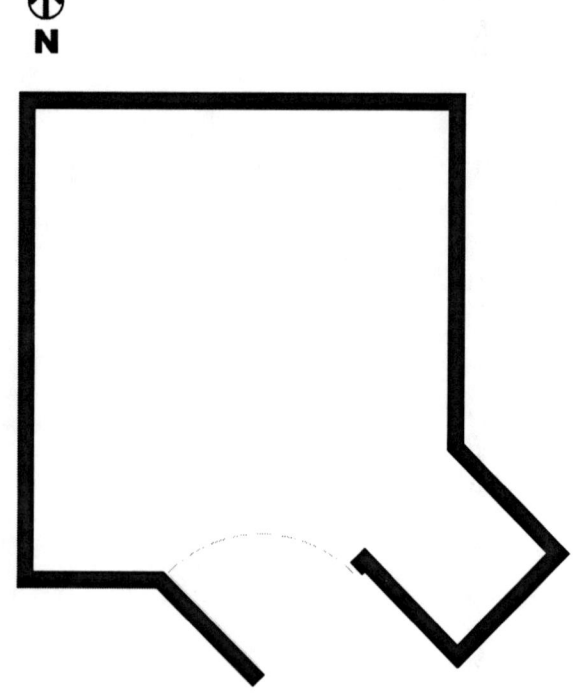

BATHROOM PLAN

SCALE: $\frac{1}{4}"=1'-0"$

LAUNDRY ROOM PLAN
SCALE: $\frac{1}{4}"=1'-0"$

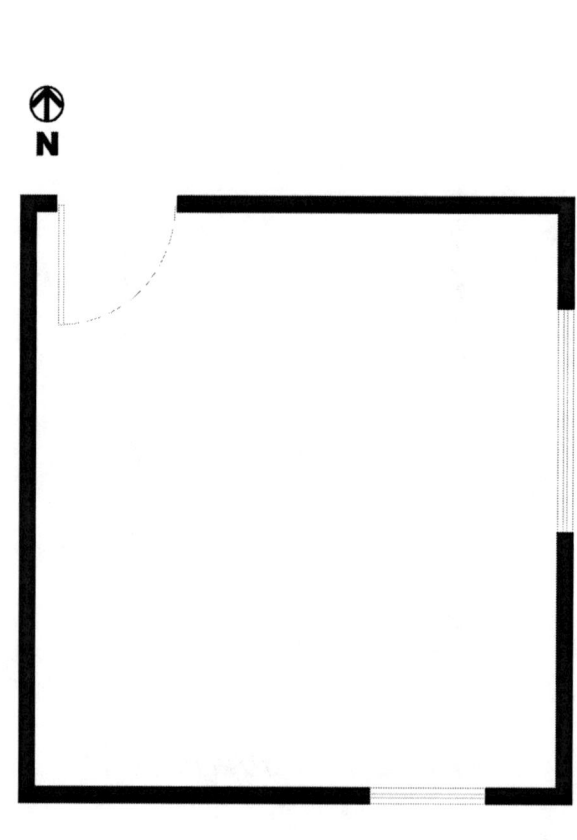

KID'S ROOM FLOOR PLAN

SCALE: $\frac{1}{4}"=1'-0"$

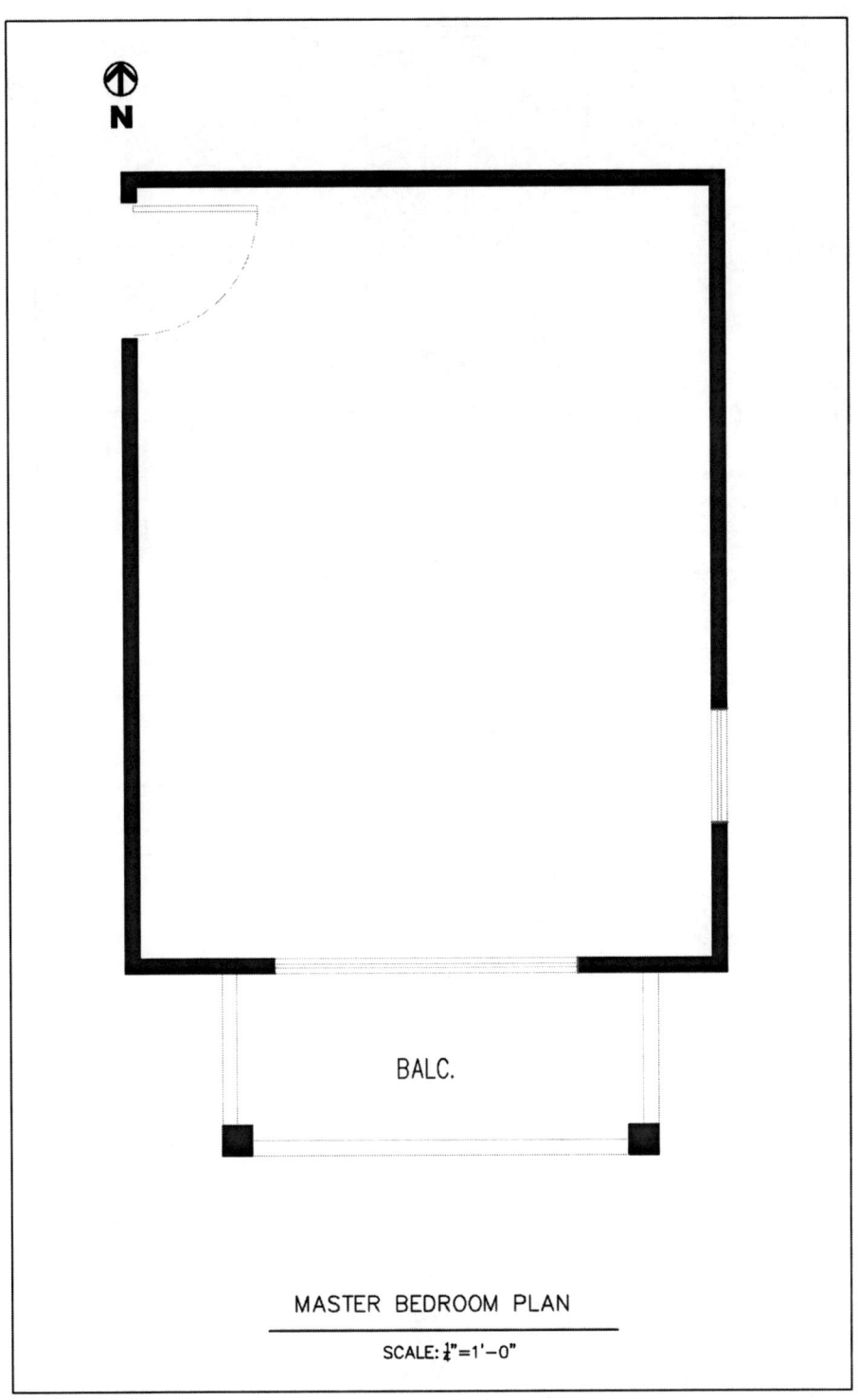

MASTER BEDROOM PLAN

SCALE: $\frac{1}{4}"=1'-0"$

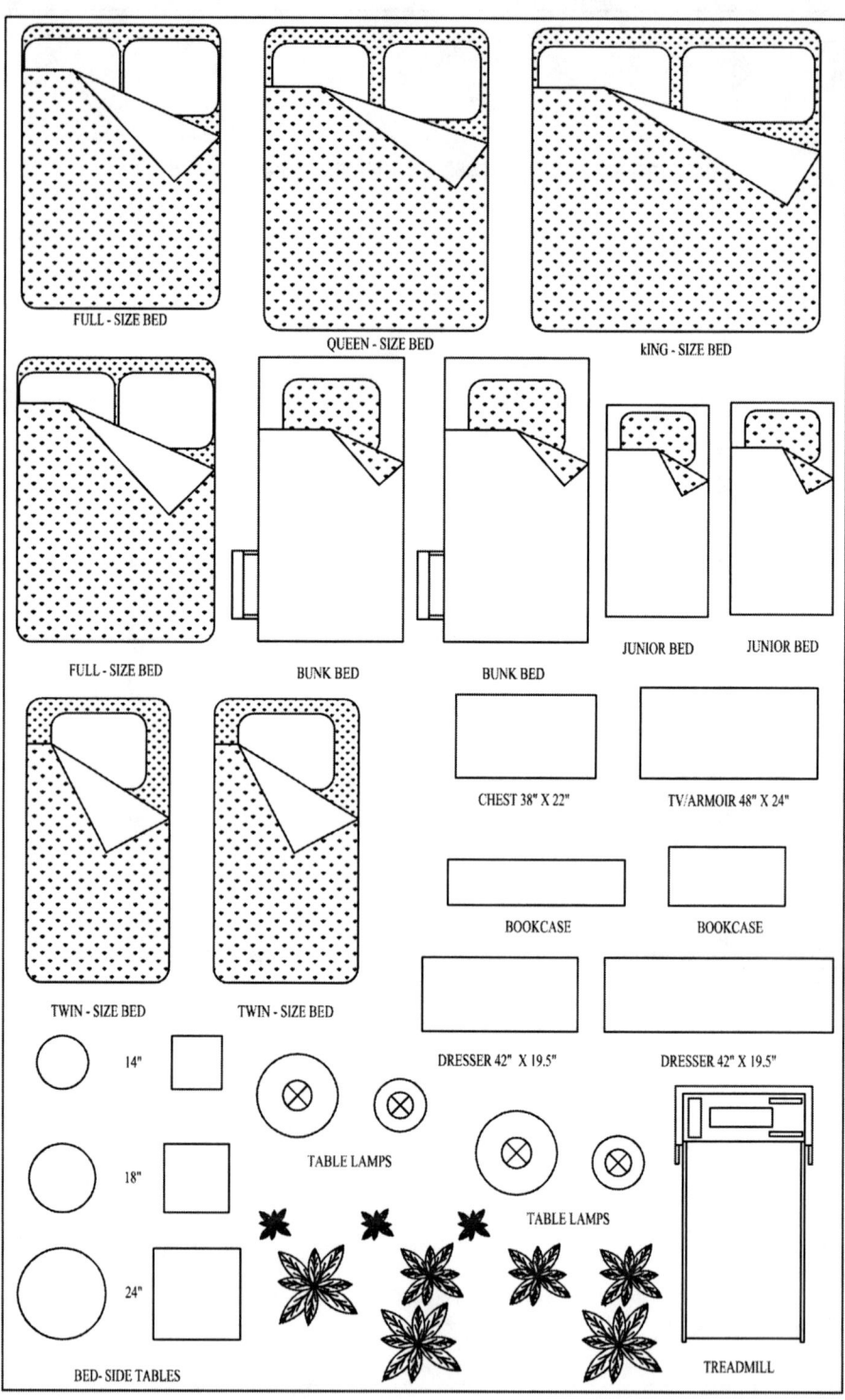

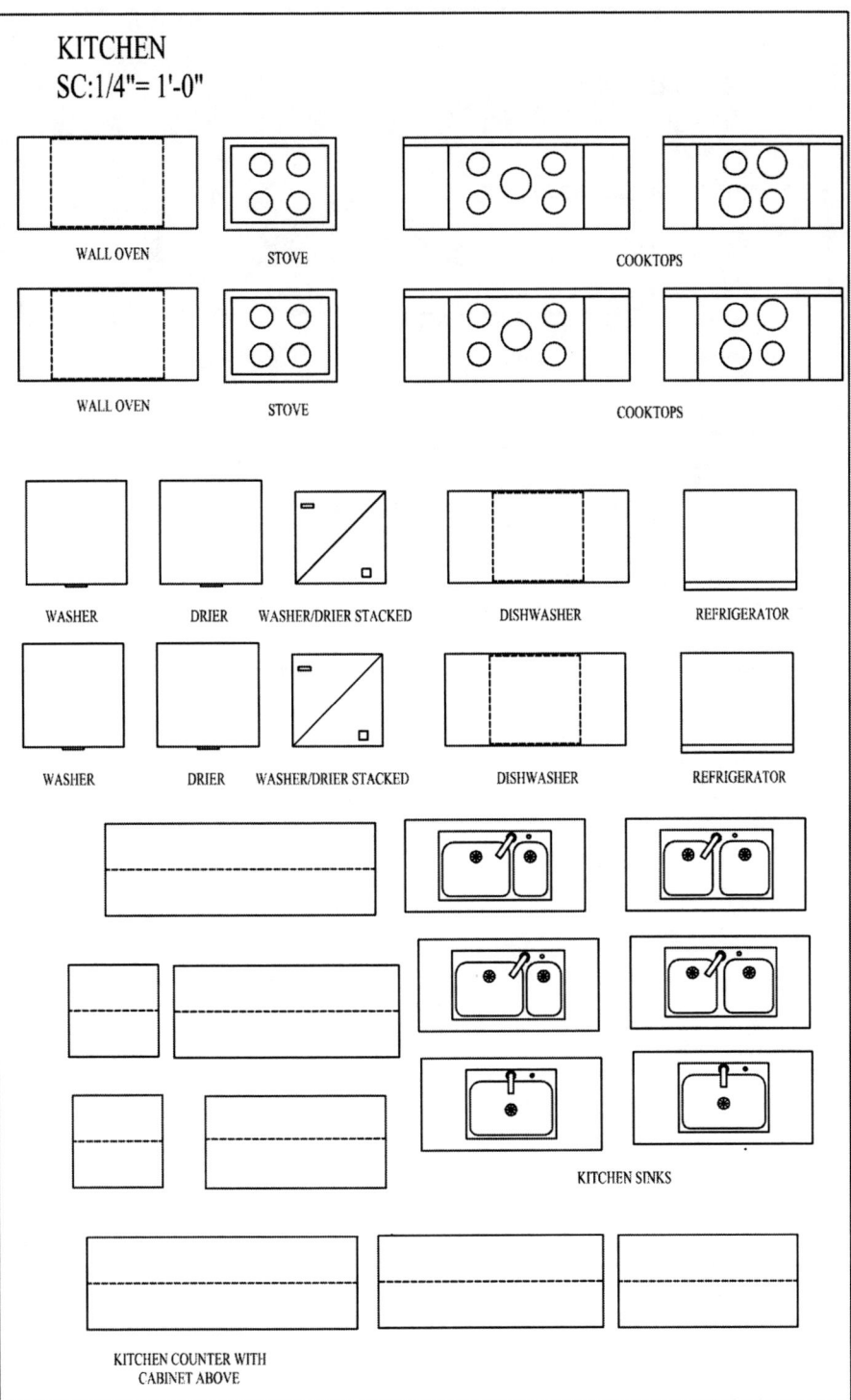

BATHROOM
SC:1/4"= 1'-0"

SHOWER BASE 36" X 36"	BATHTUB	SHOWER BASE 34" X 34"	

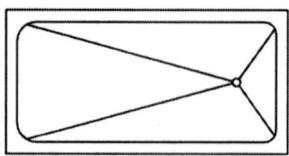 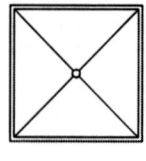 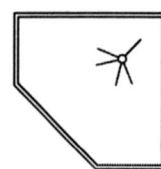

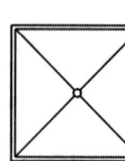 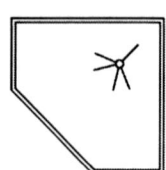

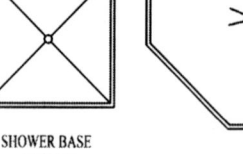

SHOWER BASE 36" X 36"   BATHTUB   SHOWER BASE 34" X 34"

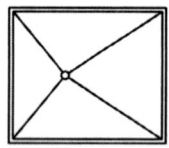 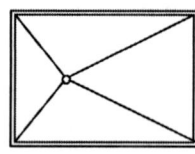 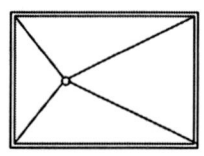

SHOWER BASE 40" X 34"   SHOWER BASE 40" X 34"   SHOWER BASE 48" X 34"   SHOWER BASE 48" X 34"

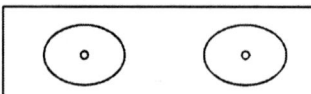 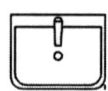 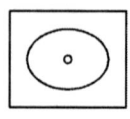 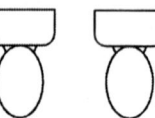

COUNTER WITH DOUBLE SINKS   PEDESTAL SINK (BASIN)   COUNTER WITH SINGLE SINK

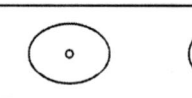 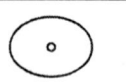 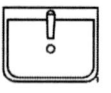 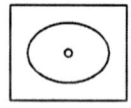 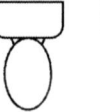 

COUNTER WITH DOUBLE SINKS   PEDESTAL SINK (BASIN)   COUNTER WITH SINGLE SINK

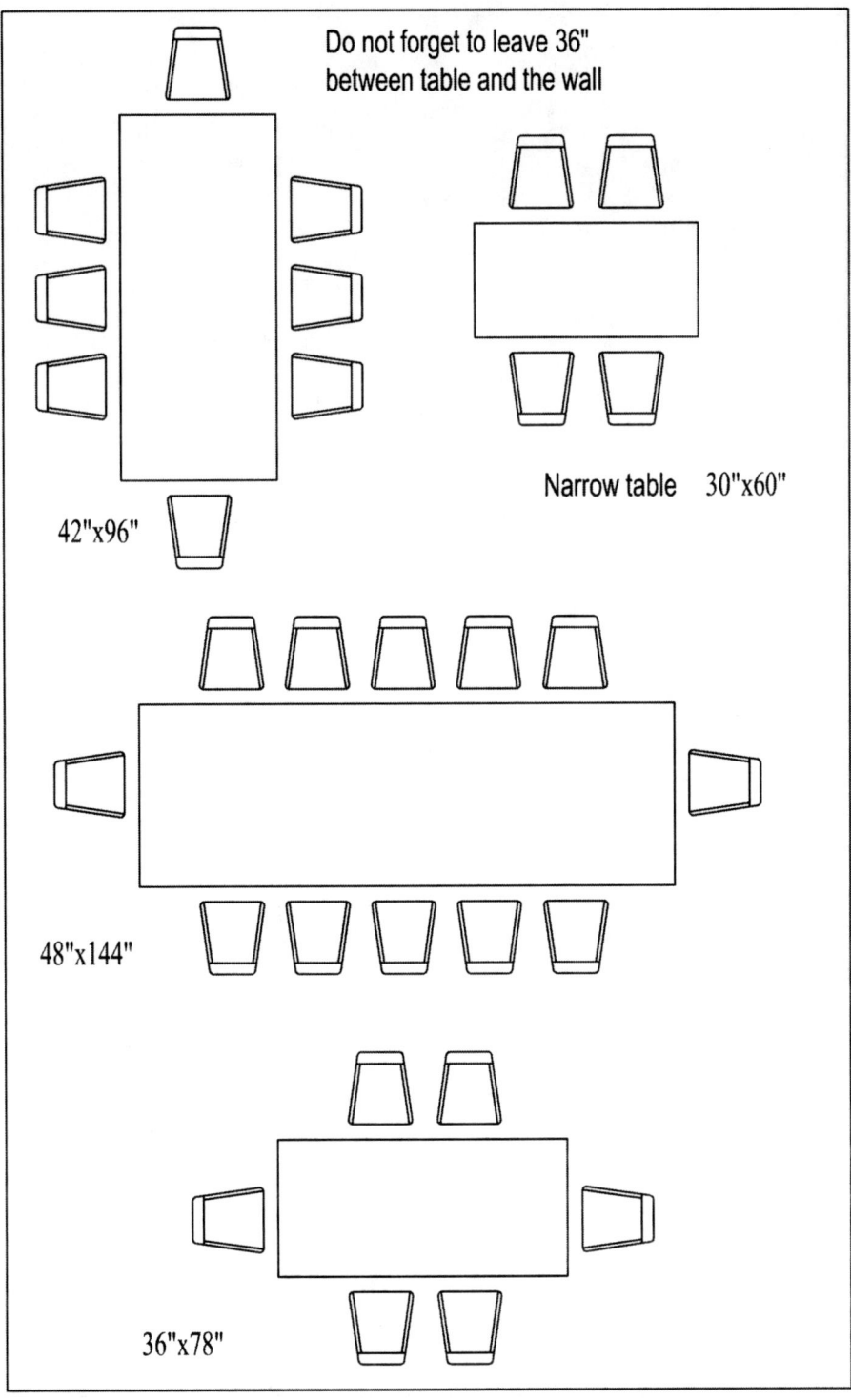

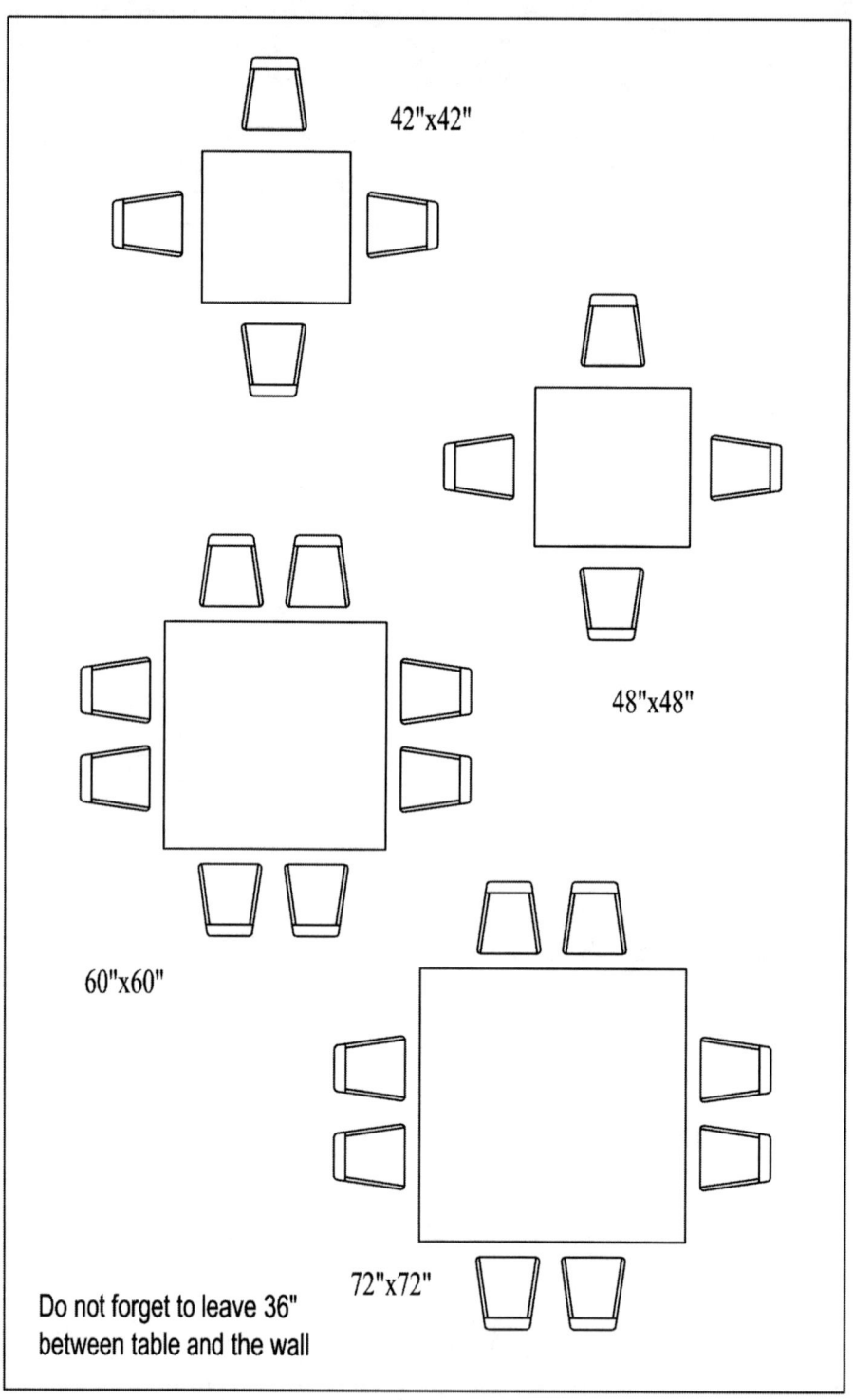

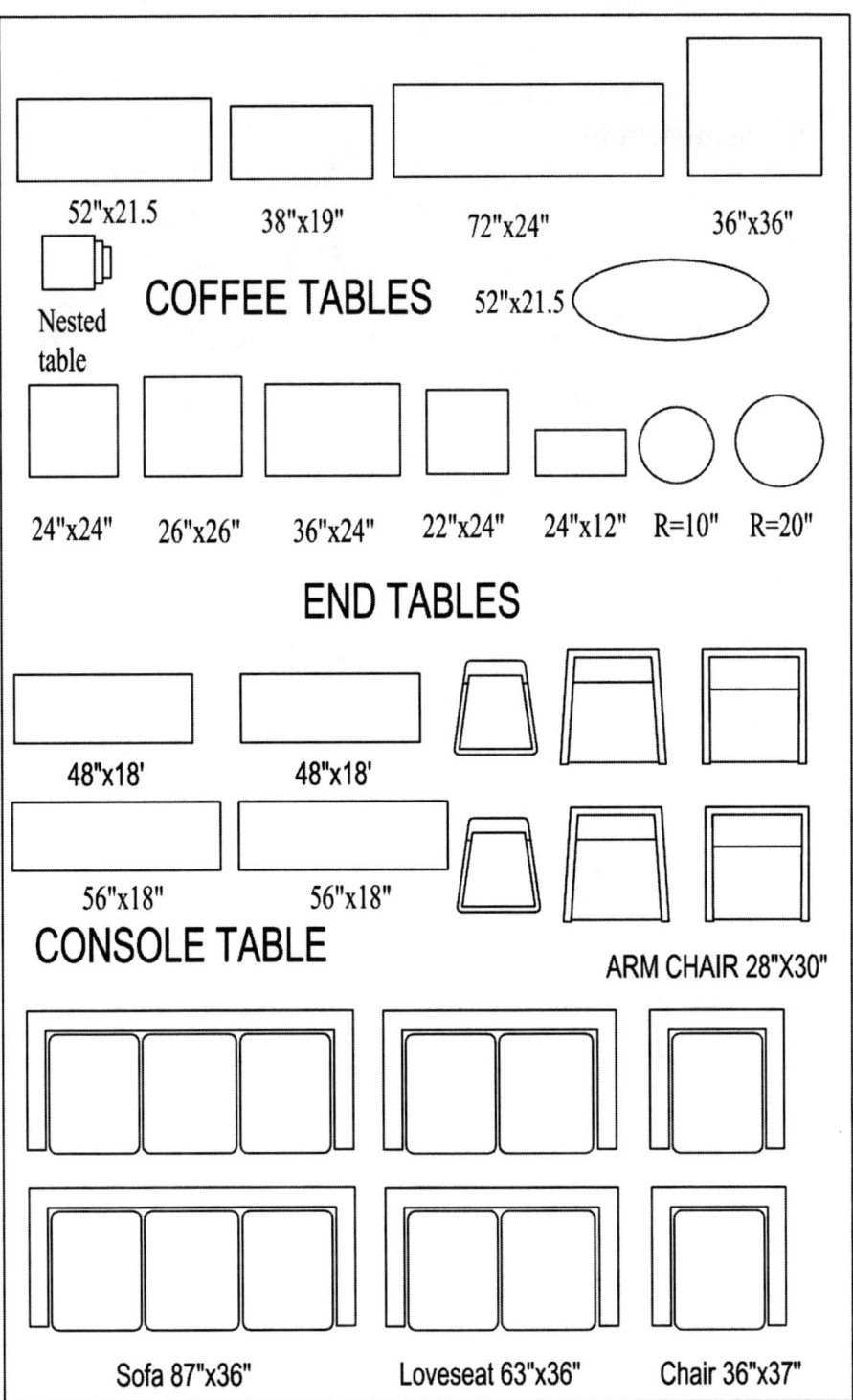

-Dashed lines are minimum clearance needed.
-Dimensions are table size.

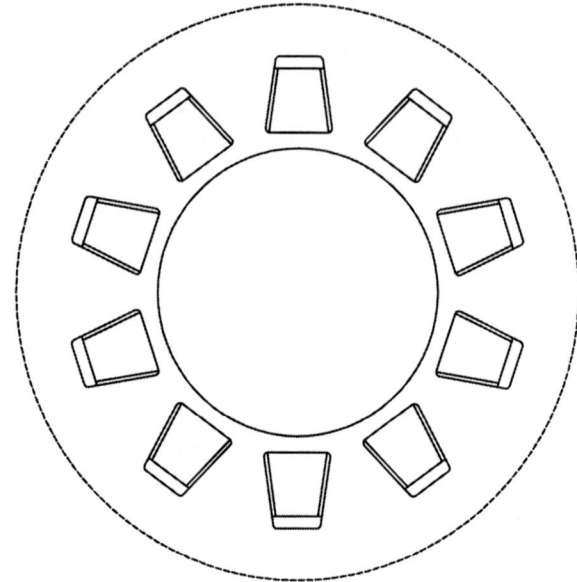

Table size.   D= 72"

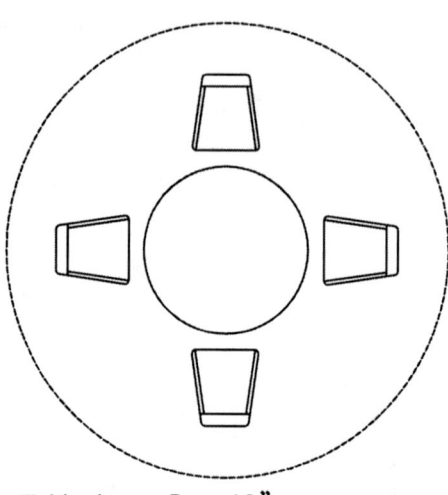

Table size.   D= 42"

-Dashed lines are minimum clearance needed.
-Dimensions are table size.

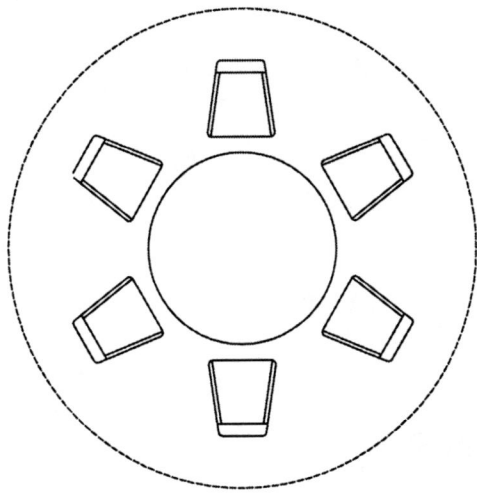

Table size.   D= 48"

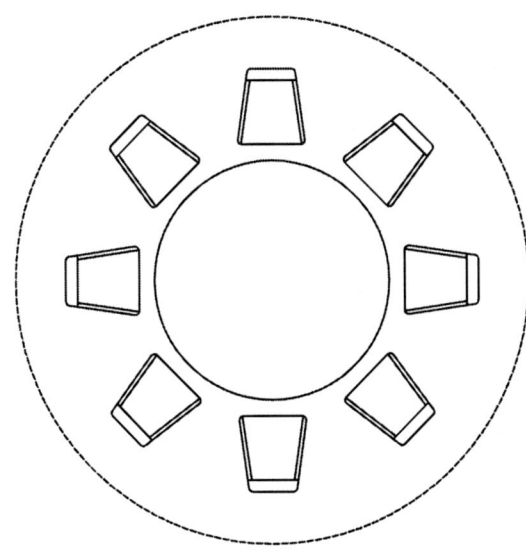

Table size.   D= 60"

Chapter 5

Final Project

The Project

A couple in their midfifties are going to downsize their home as their two children finished their university, found good jobs in other cities, and moved out.

They bought a two-bedroom apartment suite in a "no pet" building and hired you to space plan the entire rooms to make them able to have their favorite interiors, keep or buy what they need for the new space, and get rid of the extras.

A floor plan is available in the scale of 1/8" = 1' – 0" (see next page.)

The Challenges and the Solutions

Challenges:

- This couple works at and from home. Although both of them need office space, they can share one workstation.
- Their children and other friends and family usually come to visit and stay for a few days. They should be able to give them sleeping space.
- They love to have a separate corner to watch TV.
- They have a king-size bed that they want to keep.
- They need double lavatory sink on vanity in master en suite.
- They prefer to have a bigger shower booth, but they don't mind keeping the existing tub.

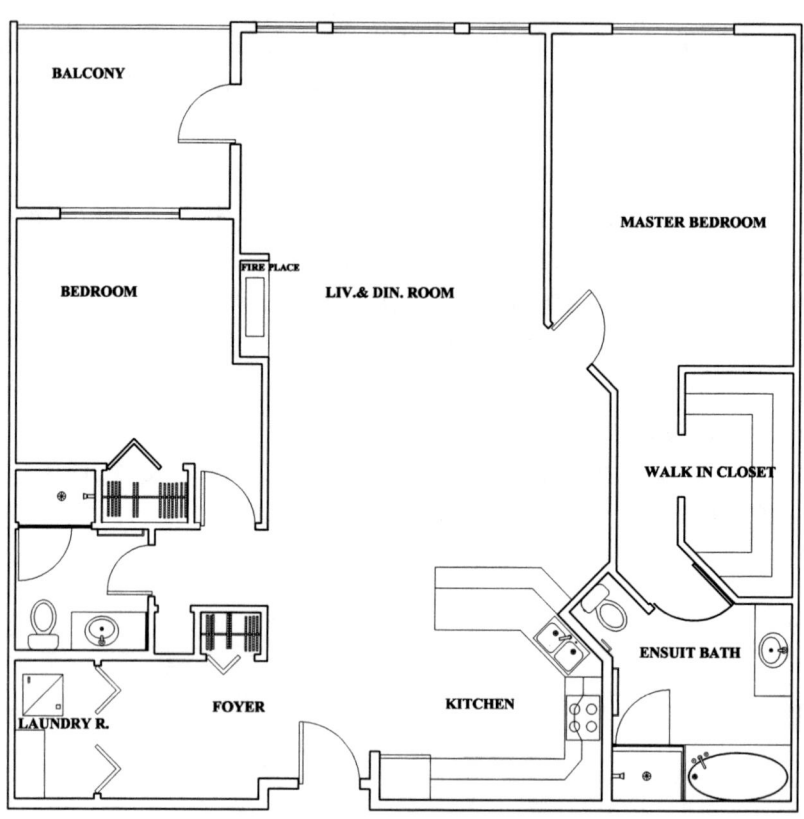

FLOOR PLAN

SCALE: 1/8" = 1'-0"

you should have a $\frac{1}{8}$"= 1'-0" furniture template or you can redraw the plan in $\frac{1}{4}$"= 1'-0" so you can use the cutouts in this book.

Solutions:

As we already discussed, there is no perfect solution for any space planning challenge; it is a matter of client's priorities, and the rest is compromising in a very professional way.

In the next pages you will see one of the plans which can be an answer to the client's needs and wants for your final project.

For furniture arrangement, we used 1/8" = 1' – 0" scale as bigger plans could not be fit in the page. You will find the 1/4" = 1' – 0" layouts of the en suite and the office as they were more challenging and needed more clarification.

En suite has a new arrangement plan for a bigger shower and a double sink without removing the tub which is time as well as money-consuming. If your client is ready to pay and can wait for a new tub or even Jacuzzi, you will have more options should to consider during the design process.

Client needs a home office as well as the guest room. The arrangement is possible by using smaller size desk and a sofa bed. Don't forget to check the size of the sofa bed when it is open. In any case, removing the chair is necessary when the bed is in use.

Another possible solution for this problem is to create a small home office workstation in front of the laundry room (corner foyer). Try it and compare the plans to find the best possible solution.

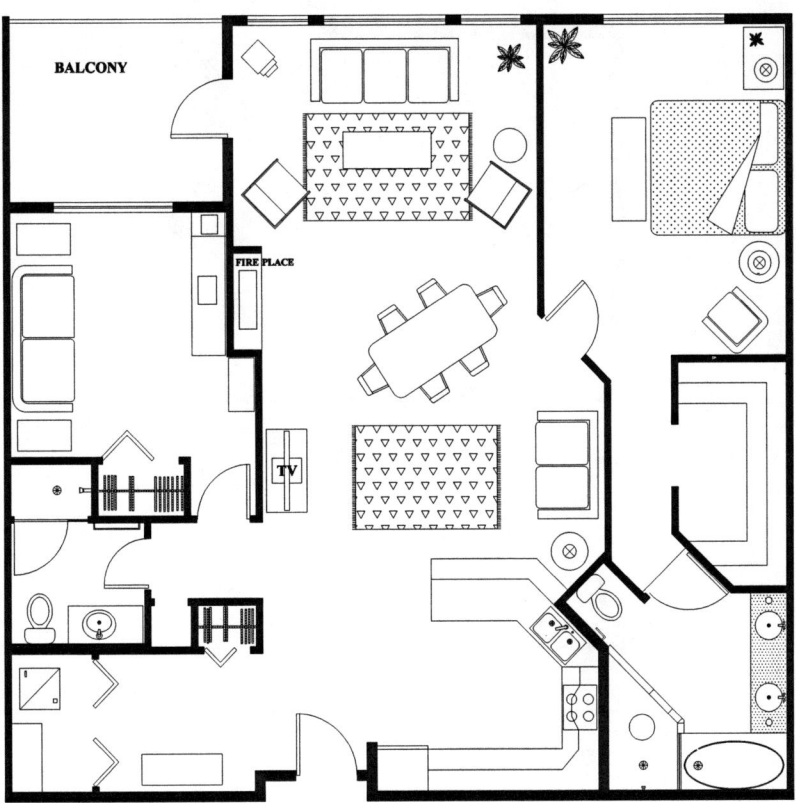

FLOOR PLAN

SCALE: 1/8" = 1'-0"

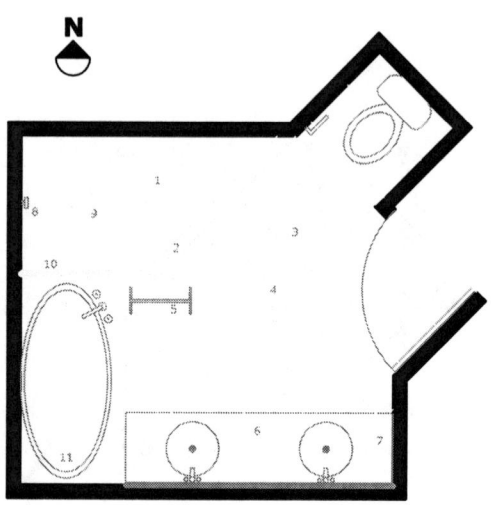

EN' SUITE FLOOR PLAN

SCALE: ¼" = 1'-0"

1- Pebbled mosaic flooring
2- glass block pony wall- H=80"
3- 16"x16" white ceramic tile
4- Chandelier
5- Towel warmer
6- silestone vanity top
7- Pendant light
8- Spray shower head on wall
9-- Rain shower head on ceiling
10- Tempered glass - H=80"
11- Exicting tub will remain the same

Design Concept:

To create a relaxing upgrade, renovated En' suit bathroom. we found the best solution with no wall turn down, the least changes in plumbing and electricity circuit while providing larger shower booth with glass block wall and two vessel sinks. chandelier in the middle and two pendants on both sides of the sinks are providing a better lighting for the space.

Design Company	
Project title	Master en'suite
Client name	
sheet#/Title	
Scale	1/4"=1'-0"

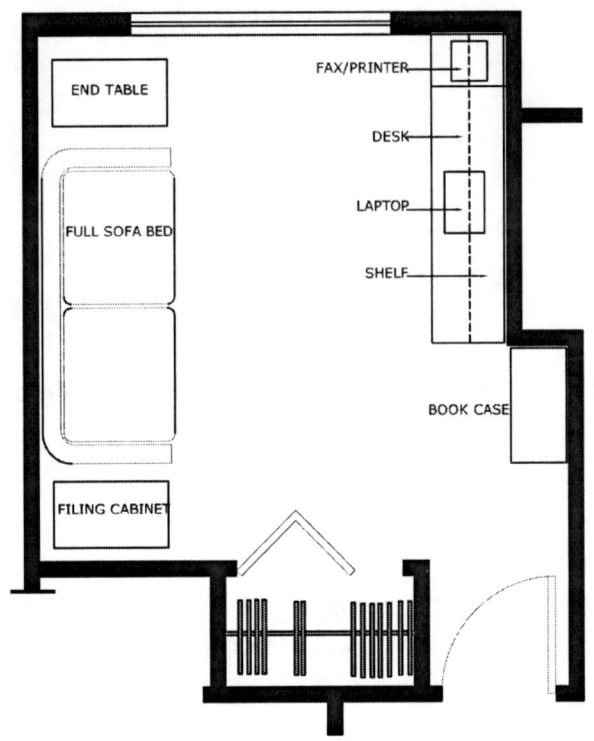

OFFICE/GUEST ROOM FLOOR PLAN

SCALE: 1/4" = 1'-0"

Design Company	
Project title	OFFICE/GUEST ROOM
Client name	
sheet#/Title	
Scale	1/4" = 1'-0"

Refrences:

- Barrier—Free Design Guide 2008 by Alberta safety code council
- Decorating Ideas That Work by Heather J. Paper
- Home Rules by Nate Berkus
- Space Planning basics by Mark Karlen
- The Element of Design—Article by Joshua David McClurg—Geneves published on August 15, 2005
- Design and colour—Article by John Lovett
- Wikipedia the free encyclopedia
- www.alibaba.com

CPSIA information can be obtained at www.ICGtesting.com
Printed in the USA
LVOW110101140212

268509LV00001B/9/P